Peace
Love

Angela
2012

Maddalena

In the midst of her Winter
lay an invincible Summer

by
Angela Chiuppi

authorHOUSE®

AuthorHouse™
1663 Liberty Drive
Bloomington, IN 47403
www.authorhouse.com
Phone: 1-800-839-8640

Published by AuthorHouse 5/9/2012

ISBN: 978-1-4685-6396-2 (e)
ISBN: 978-1-4685-6397-9 (hc)
ISBN: 978-1-4685-6398-6 (sc)

Library of Congress Control Number: 2012905053

Cover Photo: Maddalena, age 16, with her first child Silia. L'Aquila, Italy in 1910.

Vasto, Italy (copyright info: RaBoe/Wikipedia,
http://creativecommons.org/licenses/by-sa/3.0/de/legalcode)

"In the midst of Winter
I finally learned
that
there was in me
an invincible Summer."

Albert Camus

Dedicated
to
my Mother, Maddalena
for her legacy of strength, courage, sacrifice
and
to
the Order of
the Sisters of Charity
of the Blessed Virgin Mary
for their ever-present support and
unfailing guidance through my
elementary and high school years.

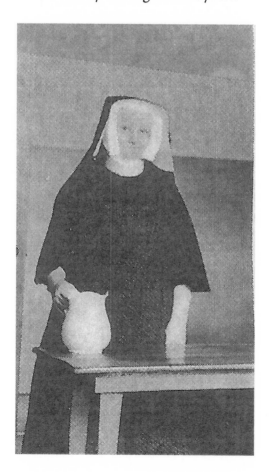

Foreword

"Behold how she was wronged!" cried out Mario Puzo about his mother in his classic book, *The Fortunate Pilgrim*. I too cry out the same words for Maddalena, my mother, who at pivotal moments in her life was forced into cruel situations where she was powerless to change the crushing circumstances placed in her path.

I am a musician, not a writer—but a ball of yarn had been occupying a large space within my spirit, growing larger and larger until it cried out for exit. The unraveling of that ball of yarn is the story of Maddalena.

I went in search of that story over a period that included fifteen trips to Italy. The village settings and the description of their cultural life are real, based on my own experience, my interviews with villagers and relatives, and the use of civil records. Especially important were interviews with Italian cousins who had first-hand knowledge of the *disgrazia* (disgrace) created by Maria Ianieri, Maddalena's mother.

This is a true story. The people, places, and events are real, and the names are accurate to the best of my ability to confirm them. Some fabrication was necessary to weave threads around the facts to bind the story together. Although the material is family history, I chose the novel form for its emotional potential. Writing it has been both joyful and painful. I trust that my family and the reader will find the book inspiring and enjoyable.

PART I

Italy

Vasto
1896

"To forget one's ancestors
is to be a brook
without a source,
a tree
without a root."

Chinese Proverb

Chapter One

"Maddalena, come back!" called out Giuseppina, her nurse, as the little three-year-old broke from her grasp and ran freely over the sandy shore of the Adriatic. Francesco and Maria smiled indulgently as they watched their firstborn child's playful escape. Their second child, Cristoforo, was comfortably ensconced in his father's arms. As was the custom, they had named the one-year-old after Francesco's father. The blue-green water lapped up on the fine sand; the sun surrounded them with a blanket of warmth; and the beauty of the seaside town of Vasto enveloped them with a sense of peace and harmony.

By now Giuseppina caught up with the child and held her under the sun-protecting umbrella. Giuseppina loved this child who would soon be leaving with her parents to return to Sella di Corno, a village nestled in the Apennine Mountains. There, Francesco's family held a contract from the Italian government to go into the mountain forests and make charcoal to be sold for heating and cooking. Francesco's business travels had brought him to Vasto where he had fallen in love with and married the beautiful daughter of the wealthy Ianieri family. Giuseppina's sadness at the impending loss of her beloved Maddalena made her tighten her hold on the child. A premonition of sorrow cast a shadow on the sunny day, as if Giuseppina knew that this would be one of the few days in Maddalena's life that the child would be free and happy.

At the end of August the family arrived in Sella di Corno. Maria saw the sprawling valleys set forth with wide swaths of golden wheat fields interspersed with soft rich green crops. After the autumn harvest, winter would swiftly move in with harsh and bitter cold. For months everything would be blanketed by snow, which would cause Maria to long for the gentler climate of her seaside home on the Adriatic. In the spring, fields of wild poppies would glow with splashes of reds and yellows.

As was the tradition, Maria and Francesco lived with Francesco's parents. Life was not easy in the Ferrara household. Francesco's father, Cristoforo, held a tight rein on his son. His stepmother, Amelia, resented the intrusion of the expanding family into her small home. Maria was now pregnant with their third child. Maria longed for the comforts of her once privileged life where a large house with many daily services made life comfortable and tranquil. She fondly remembered mornings when the hairdresser came to arrange everyone's hair, and the seamstresses came to measure and sew their clothes. She remembered the dinners with the beautiful tablecloths which had been hung in a special room so they would have no creases in them. She missed Giuseppina, Maddalena's nurse and caretaker, who had adored the child and was unable to join them.

She cringed as her thoughts were pulled back to the present where the animals lived on the ground level of the home, where charcoal was stored in the second level, and where the family was crammed into the small rooms on the third level.

But more than her physical surroundings, she, who had spent her days learning to embroider, walking on the beach, or reading, was now required to do heavy manual labor. She dreaded the spring after the snow had melted and plans began for the first caravan into the mountains. Turning bark into charcoal was a process that required days of hard labor. Maria shuddered as she remembered her first time. She had almost died that year.

She could still see the men, and a few women, gathering to start the trip. The women had prepared food for the trip while the men packed mules with equipment for cooking meals, cutting the bark from the trees, and making stakes for cooking the bark into charcoal. The caravan began its climb into the mountains with both loaded-down mules and able-bodied people sharing the load. She had thought it would never end, that steady upward climb, even though there were occasional stops for food and rest. The worst part was settling in for the night—sleeping on a rough mat on the ground, the cold penetrating deep into the interior of her bones. The following days continued the nightmare.

"Maria," the harsh voice of Amelia interrupted her thoughts, "get these children out of here for awhile." Amelia was particularly resentful of having young children disturb her peace and quiet. Maria saw Maddalena's soft brown eyes widen with fear. A sensitive spirit, the child cringed as her step-grandmother spoke. Cristoforo simply clung to his mother's side. Maria, without a response, quickly gathered the children and left the room. As they walked down the narrow outside stairway to the ground level, she spoke to the children gently and cheerfully. "We're going to the piazza where you can run and play."

Sella di Corno's piazza consisted of a small square with a traditional fountain in the center where the women came for water and to gossip. After visiting, they filled their *concas* (large copper-vessels with handles), hoisted them onto their heads and walked home with the afternoon supply of water. Since there was no indoor plumbing, a trip to the well occurred two or three times a day, depending on the size of the family. The children played as mothers gathered the water. Michele, the baby, sat with Maria. Maddalena and Cristoforo quickly joined with the others, and soon forgot the angry sound of Amelia's voice. Maria did not. Amelia's recent command brought back memories of her first caravan trip into the mountains like a splash of cold water in her face. Full of criticism and haranguing, that nightmare replayed in her mind much as she sought to forget it.

She remembered that once the caravan reached its permanent location for the charcoal processing, they set up tents. The women stacked and stored the food supplies and began preparations for the meal to follow. The main meal had to include a combination of ingredients that would provide the men with a well rounded, fortified single dish to meet the needs of their heavy labor. Diced *pancetta* (Italian bacon) and garlic were browned in olive oil, while spaghetti was cooked *al dente* (to the tooth or firm to the bite). Chickens in cages had been carried in the caravan to provide the eggs to complete the dish. While draining the spaghetti, some hot water was set aside. Once the spaghetti and *pancetta* were mixed together, the extra hot water was tossed into the combined ingredients and immediately the raw eggs were added. This recipe gave birth to *pasta alla carbonara* (*carbona* meaning charcoal made from wood).

After preparing the meal, the women were also expected to help carry bark hacked off the trees by the men and stack it at the burning pit. These pits were large holes dug into the ground and covered with a teepee shaped structure using long branches with foliage as stakes. Once the teepee was covered with leaves and moss to prevent the smoke from escaping, a fire was lit and kept at a low heat while the pieces of bark were laid crosswise until they filled the hole. The low fire cooked the bark which turned it into charcoal. The next day, when the charcoal was ready, the teepee was removed and the charcoal loaded and strapped down on the mules for the long trip down the mountain and back to town.

Maria's eyes filled with tears as she recalled the women's sarcastic comments when, after days of hard labor, she could no longer move her cramped, aching muscles. "Oh, Francesco, what kind of a wife have you picked?" one of the women said. The derision only made Francesco angry with her, and she had longed for death to end the nightmare. She was sustained on the trip down the mountain only by the thought of seeing her beloved children again. When she arrived home, she had lain in bed for three days with a high fever—unable to move from exhaustion.

"Mamma, Mamma," Cristoforo called out, toddling on his little three-year-old legs as he came across the piazza. Seeing his carefree face pulled Maria from her memories. Holding the year old Michele, she grabbed Cristoforo as he jumped onto her lap. A surge of joy swept over her as she held him close. Maddalena was still off chasing birds that came close to the fountain for a drink. Maria's children were everything to her, especially since Francesco had grown cold and frustrated with her.

The late afternoon mountain air had turned chilly. She called Maddalena to her and made her way back to the house. With a heavy heart she began to climb up the narrow stairway.

Francesco looked up as they came into the room. He felt heartsick at the change in Maria's face. When they first met, he had fallen in love with her gentle beauty expressed through her warm brown eyes, quick smile and lilting laughter that bubbled in her sweet voice. Now her features were drawn into a tight knot and she hardly ever smiled. He knew she had felt the sting of Amelia's wrath that he and his father were also wary of. The townspeople had not been kind either and though he had been loath to do so, he too berated her for things he knew she could not help. He felt trapped. The first time she told him she could not survive another caravan trip, he had allowed her to return to Vasto to rest and visit her family. He recalled how her brother Luigi had written that she did not want to return. She had pleaded to remain until the following spring when she would have had time to regain her strength. He had consented, but when she returned nothing had changed.

Maria set the children down and went to the kitchen to help prepare the evening meal. Michele immediately began to cry and Francesco picked him up to sooth him. Cristoforo and Maddalena played together quietly on the floor. As he gazed at his three children, Francesco's thoughts drifted back to a time before they were born.

It had been the fall of 1891 when Francesco first met the Ianieri family. Maria's aging father had just turned over his business affairs to his eldest child, Luigi, who then became the surrogate father for the remaining ten children. According to Italian custom, the eldest son would inherit the family resources. In turn, he would become responsible for the boys until they found work or entered the military and for the girls until husbands were found for them. Should the girls remain unmarried, he was expected to support them for the rest of their lives. When the young, handsome Francesco had asked for the 15-year-old Maria's hand, simply the fact that he had a business was sufficient for Luigi to grant his request. A substantial dowry was offered, which included a house with land and orchards in Vasto, and a certain amount of gold. The generous offer was accepted although Francesco knew he was tied to his father's charcoal business where he was sorely needed. A move to Vasto would be impossible. It never crossed his mind that once married, Maria would have to become a part of the family business, as was expected of married women. All the women helped with the yearly caravan. As he reflected on that happy time, remembering the delicate, soft, protected Maria, he realized the enormity of the problem that faced them both.

Francesco was miserable. He loved Maria but the forces around him pulled at him—his father's lack of understanding, his stepmother's downright hostility and the vicious gossip of the villagers. Jealously they made comments such as, "*Se porta come una regina*" (she acts like a queen). Francesco had finally succumbed and often scolded Maria, "Why can't you be like the others?"

"Papa! Papa!" screamed Cristoforo. Maddalena had taken his toy and would not give it back. Setting Michele down, Francesco walked over to the two children who were now both yelling and tugging at the toy.

Amelia called from the kitchen in her shrill angry voice, "Francesco, do something and make them be quiet." Maria continued with her meal preparation, knowing she could not drop everything to comfort Cristoforo.

"*Nonno*," (grandfather) Maddalena called as she gave up the fight and ran to the door. "*Nonno*," she cried again as she threw herself into her grandfather's arms. He picked her up, his warm heart responding with joy to this sweet child.

"*Piccina*" (little one), "*piccina mia*" (my little one) he softly spoke into her ear. By now Cristoforo, too, had forgotten his toy and was pulling on Nonno's pant leg. Michele had returned to his father's lap and was content. Francesco looked at his three children and felt a warm glow of satisfaction. The moment was interrupted when Amelia called everyone to dinner.

Early the next morning Maria set off for her daily trip to shop for food. While Michele slept, she took Cristoforo and Maddalena down the long narrow stairway and crossed the street. Passing several row houses, she stopped in front of the village's only general grocery store and mini-restaurant. Above the entry way the letters "*VINO*" indicated that wine was also sold and served. She parted the hanging beaded ropes used to keep the flies out when the door was open and entered.

"*Buon giorno*, Maria," the voice of Andrea Chiuppi, the storeowner, greeted her. A sense of relief flowed through her when she realized he was at the counter. She had dreaded the possibility that Massimo, Andrea's son, might be on duty today. The times he waited on her left her shaken. He alternated from an angry shouting at her when she couldn't make up her mind to a nasty set of comments with sexual innuendoes. He seemed to enjoy her discomfort, and she often cut short her shopping to get away from him.

Maddalena's voice interrupted her thoughts. She had seen the cookies in the display case and was tapping the glass with both hands while jumping up and down. "*Va bene*," Maria said to Andrea, indicating it was all right for him to give her one.

Andrea liked Maria. He felt sad for her as he watched her suffer the isolation from the women in the town and the derision of her husband. He also respected the Ferrara family particularly since their charcoal business provided the townspeople jobs that were hard to come by. He and his wife, Carolina, had opened the store to eke out a living for themselves and their five children. They had worked very hard for years and now that Massimo was an adult, they hoped some of the burden would become lighter. Even though they had sent him away to learn to be a tailor, there was very little call for a tailor in Sella di Corno.

Andrea and Carolina were disappointed in their son. Massimo flew into rages over nothing. When this happened he took it out on the merchandise, tearing down the cheeses and salamis hanging in the store and sometimes pushing his mother out of his way. Andrea, who had lost one leg in a mountain accident, was physically unable to control his son. He was puzzled. Known in the village as *Andrea, le bon* (Andrew, the good one), he had always been mild-mannered and gentle. Carolina, his wife, was a strong, hard-working woman who not only helped run the store but also knitted and crocheted articles, which she sold. The Chiuppi family was highly respected by the townspeople. Their son, however, was looked down on for his bad treatment of his mother and his inexplicable outbursts of anger. Although he was of marriageable age, no families would entrust their daughters to marry him.

Maria, having felt the brunt of his personality in the past, hastened to complete the day's shopping before he might show up. After paying Andrea, she gathered up the children, who were happily munching on their *pizzelle* (a waffle-like cookie, which was the town's specialty), and went back through the doorway into the street. As she began her journey back, she looked down the street to the three-story, gray stucco building she called home. It sat at an angle at the corner where the street made a turn. The side of the building facing her had no windows—just a bare, grim hard wall. She felt tightness in her chest as if the windows of her life had been ripped out and there was no air for her to breathe. Her life too had become bare, grim and gray. She felt empathy for the building trapped into a corner forever. By now she had reached the stairway. The children did not want to go up. Neither did Maria. They cried to go to the piazza and see the birds.

Maria loved being in the piazza with the children. It was a pleasure to watch them enjoy the freedom of childhood, running and laughing with each other. It always touched her to see Maddalena being protective of her little brother when the older children shoved him out of their way. She was especially happy to see Maddalena playing with the two sisters, Felicetta and Assunta. They were about the same age and had become close friends. Felicetta, the older sister, was quiet, plump and slow moving with a round face and gentle eyes. Assunta, on the other hand, was lively and slender, with a pointed chin, dark curly hair and dancing eyes. It pleased Maria to see that the moment Maddalena got to the piazza, the two sisters raced over to her, calling out, "Maddalena,

Maddalena, come see this new game." Maria could not know it then, but this friendship would last a lifetime.

"No—not now," Maria told the children, "we must go and see Michele." She shepherded them up the narrow stairway as she balanced the bags of groceries on her arm. They reached the third level and entered the kitchen door. She barely put the groceries down before Michele jumped into her arms.

"*Amore*" (my love), she whispered in his ear as she hugged him tightly. He was the most fragile of her three children and the least demanding. She worried about him but there was little time to dwell on it, especially now, when Francesco had to prepare for his yearly business travel, to get orders for the charcoal. The summer months were the easiest for travel, and it was already June.

She had begged Francesco to let her and the children go with him to Vasto and remain there for the winter, but he had rejected the idea completely. She became deeply depressed thinking about the upcoming winter and the caravan the following spring. An icy fear chilled her to the bone—could she survive it again? If not, what would happen to her children?

"Francesco," she had pleaded, "the winter is too hard on the children—cooped up in these small rooms with Nonna Amelia constantly upbraiding them. When they are a little older it will be easier for them to tolerate. "Besides," she had added, "the sea air would be so good for Michele's health. You know how much he suffers from the cold."

"*Fa la finita*" (the subject is closed), he had curtly answered. Her heart sank but she could say no more—for the time being, at least. She would bide her time and find the right moment. That night at the dinner table, Francesco discussed the trip with his father. When Vasto was mentioned, Maria was stunned as she heard Amelia say, "Why not take Maria and the children with you to visit their grandparents?" Maria held her breath as she watched father and son exchange looks of surprise. It was clear to them that Amelia was suggesting it not to benefit Maria and the children, but to give herself the peace and quiet she wanted. Cristoforo would not cross his wife and Francesco would not cross his father so the deed was done. Cristoforo turned to his son and said, "Good idea—it will be good for everyone."

Maria could hardly breathe. She sat in an eager silence. Could it be? Could it really be? To go back to sea breezes off the beautiful blue-green Adriatic? To go back to the mild winter? To go back to the warmth of her family? Her heart sang a silent song, but outwardly she gave no indication of her feelings.

Chapter Two

It was the late spring of 1900. Maria and the children were still in Vasto. In Sella di Corno, the sheepherders were making preparations for their annual trip to Rome. The village offered very little opportunity to make money. They would guide their flocks down the mountainside, onto the plains and eventually to the fields outside the city, where they would begin their transactions with the Romans. It was a grueling trip which would include carrying food and supplies, as well as tents and bedding for the seven days it took to walk there. After they arrived and the pregnant sheep gave birth, the Romans eagerly bought up the lambs—most to be eaten as young as possible, a delicacy called *abbacchio*, and a few to be raised for their wool. When the weeks it took to complete the transactions passed, the sheepherders began the long trip back to Sella di Corno. The return trip took longer. As soon as they reached the foothills of the Apennines they began the ascent to Sella di Corno. The money they earned would help them buy the wood or charcoal they needed for cooking and heating in the winter.

Other ways the families supported themselves included keeping a cow or goat for milk and planting vegetable gardens. The garden often included root vegetables which were stored in cellars for the winter. Those lucky enough to own a piece of land large enough to grow wheat were able to barter with their neighbors. Everyone who was able searched the mountains for wild strawberries, hazelnuts and mushrooms and collected herbs for seasoning and treating illnesses.

Staples and supplies were purchased at the only general store in town, which was run by the Chiuppi family.

Consequently, everyone in Sella di Corno knew the Chiuppi family. The store was often tended by Andrea or Carolina, or by one of their older children, Massimo, Bettina, or Anna Felice. Aside from the parents, Bettina was everyone's favorite. Her soft voice and gentle manner encouraged the villagers to talk about their problems. They felt she listened and responded with a kind heart. Unfortunately she had recently married and moved to Tornimparte, a village a full day's walk away. Anna Felice, her younger sister, was capable, courteous and all business, so customers' needs were met, but not with the same warmth they had with Bettina. Bettina was missed. No one wanted to be served by Massimo, the oldest brother. He was hostile and rude, particularly to women. The younger son, Giulio, was nine and was already showing signs of following in his older brother's footsteps. Carolina, their mother, was again pregnant.

The women of the village talked about all of this at the fountain. The activities of the town were hashed and rehashed as they gathered together to re-fill their empty *concas*. The Chiuppi family was often a dominant thread woven into their daily discussions.

"Can you believe it?" Concetta exclaimed, "my Rosa is in love with that Massimo. Of course, he is a handsome devil—I don't mind looking at him myself, but I told her looking is all she can do."

"That's true," chimed in the other women.

"He's probably the best looking man in the whole village," continued Chiarina.

"Well," Concetta went on, "I had a fight with Antonio over the matter.

"Look, Concetta," he said to me, "why not let her marry him? He has a business, hasn't he? She would be well taken care of."

"*Che stupido* (how stupid) you are," I told him, "for a piece of bread you would give your daughter over to a man who mistreats his own mother and can't control his temper?—No!—she remains with her family until we find a good-hearted, kind man who will treat her right—even if she stays home for the rest of her life."

"You're right, Concetta," he finally answers me, 'but maybe he will change."

"Never," I answered him, 'a leopard does not change his spots. The matter is ended."

"But how about Rosa?" asked Chiarina.

"Don't worry," answered Concetta, "Rosa is a good girl with a head on her shoulders. She will listen."

As they prepared to leave the piazza, Luisa hurriedly called them back together. Luisa knew more than anyone because her father delivered the mail. Her breath came in short gasps as she could hardly contain herself to tell them the latest news, "Francesco got another letter from Vasto today, and he's walking around with a sour face. My father says Maria probably doesn't want to come back again."

"Well, that's nothing new. That's what happened last time, remember?" said Concetta, "he had to actually go and get her and bring her back himself."

"Yes, she thinks she's too good for us," they chimed in together.

"You know," Luisa added, "it would make Amelia happy if she never showed up again."

"What do you think Francesco will do?" asked Chiarina.

They all rolled their eyes to heaven, shrugging their shoulders as they set their *concas* on their heads and walked out of the piazza.

Chapter Three

The Adriatic Sea glowed in the afternoon sun. Maria watched as the three children alternated playing in the sand and wading in the water. The sea air had brought color to Michele's cheeks. Maria too had felt a renewal of strength and energy. She tried not to think of Sella di Corno, but her daily arguments with her brother Luigi about going back were like a thorn in her heart. Missing Francesco was another thorn. She loved him—knowing that his turning on her was not his true feeling but a result of the pressures from his parents and the villagers. And yet, she could not go back—she would not go back.

"It will be my death," she thought. Her younger brothers and sisters were delighted to have her home and enjoyed playing with the children. She could see two of them coming down the hill to join her and the children. As she watched them, her eyes took in the small village perched above the sea. The colors splashed before her like a painter's palette—homes painted burnt sienna, mustard, and pink, dotted with tall dark green cypress, coral tiled roofs and flowering bushes. It was her village, Vasto, and it sat like a queen on a throne peacefully watching over her Adriatic domain.

By now her siblings had arrived and thrown themselves at her, hugging her then pulling her up from her chair and dancing around her. "Maria, Maria," they shouted, "*Babbo*"(Daddy) says to come home. It's time to get ready for dinner." They scampered off to get their nieces and nephews out of the water while Maria folded the chair and umbrella. She had not noticed how quickly the afternoon had passed.

When she walked in the door, she knew. Luigi looked determined and her father looked sad. Luigi waved a letter at her and said, "Francesco has arranged for you to go home." The warmth of the afternoon sun she had carried in with her turned to a bitter cold. She could not speak. His words had fallen on her like a death sentence.

It was the last week of June. It was the best time of year for the difficult journey to Sella di Corno. She thought of Maddalena's recent birthday. She had just turned seven and had reveled in her seashore celebration. Giuseppina had made all her favorite delicacies. The little one who loved the sea and basked in the doting attention of her beloved nurse would now face again the bitter winter of Sella di Corno and the even more devastating cold of her step-grandmother.

Maria felt gripped by a vise that tightened every aspect of her being. Finally Luigi broke through the silence, saying, "Your place is with your husband. The children's place is with their father. You cannot bring disgrace upon the family and remain here separated from your husband."

His voice was hard and his words pummeled her like rocks hitting from all sides. Still she did not speak.

"Maria," her father interjected, "I know how hard this is for you. I am sorry that it has turned out this way but Luigi is right. A woman belongs with her husband. You must make the best of it, *"cara mia"* (my dear).

It hurt him to see the pain in her face. She was his first-born daughter, the second child in a family of eleven children. He cherished her and had rejoiced in the good catch she had made with the handsome businessman from Sella di Corno. He had been concerned about her fragility but had been reassured by Francesco's solidity and devotion.

Still she could not speak. Luigi was irritated with her silence and immobility. "Giuseppina will help you pack. You leave in the morning," he said flatly and walked out of the room.

Her father came to her side and placed his hand on her shoulder. *"Cara,"* he said, his voice carrying the message of his love, "you will be all right, I'm sure. *"Coraggio,"* (courage)—you must be strong. Come, let us have dinner and then go to Giuseppina and get started."

That night, after Luigi left to join his friends for coffee at the local bar in the piazza, she went back to her father. "*Babbo*, I will need extra money for the trip in case of trouble," she finally spoke.

His face filled with love, he reached out for her hand. "Here," he said, "I had already planned it. Also, take this gold ring that had been your mother's."

His love broke through the locked gate to her heart, and tears flowed freely.

"*Babbo! Babbo*! What will become of me?" she sobbed in his arms. He held her gently until she was quiet. She finally pulled away and in a broken voice said, "I must help Giuseppina pack."

Giuseppina had already done most of the packing. Continuing to work, her face reflecting her anguish, Giuseppina asked, "*Signora*, why can't I come with you? It's too hard a trip for a woman alone with three little children."

"Oh, Giuseppina, if only that could be. It would make me and the children so happy. But the Sella di Corno villagers would never accept it, and besides, there is no room in the house we live in." she answered.

The next morning, the buggy was ready. The household had gathered at the front entrance. Giuseppina had packed them a lunch with a special package for the children filled with sweets.

"Safe journey, *amore*," her father whispered in her ear as he embraced her.

"Mamma, Mamma, let's go," the children called, as they ran around the two restless horses. Maria's gaze fell on the sad faces of her brothers and sisters, the hard face of Luigi, and the stricken faces of her father and Giuseppina, and she walked to the buggy.

After settling the children, who held tightly to Giuseppina's special package, she gave one long, last look at her loved ones and told the driver to go.

The die was cast.

Chapter Four

The journey was difficult. Although they stopped and spent the nights in inns along the way, the children became increasingly restless and tired. Maddalena sometimes sat next to the driver as the buggy bounced along rough roads on the way to Sella di Corno. When Cristoforo, now five, and Michele, three years old, napped, Maria's thoughts could fully dwell on the plan she had conceived in her desperation. Could she? Would she? She agonized as her mind went over and over the possibilities. No matter what action she would take, she was tormented by the results. On the one hand, her heart would die and on the other, her body. She knew Francesco loved his children and so did Cristoforo, their grandfather. With this in mind, she made her decision. She tried not to think of Amelia.

On the last morning of the trip, a summer storm kept them from resuming their journey. The children reveled in the freedom of running around the inn. This delay would have them arriving in Sella di Corno late that night.

"Better for my plan," thought Maria. She shuddered at the thought. Her body felt hot and then cold. She tried not to look at the children. She felt her mind could not stand the torment, that it would snap. Beginning to shake all over, she worked to pull herself together. The children's demands on her helped to re-focus her attention and bring back some semblance of control over her emotions.

As the night descended and they were close to Sella di Corno, she was filled with terror. She was about to do the unthinkable. She was glad the children slept. Again, she did not want to look at them. She signaled the driver to stop so she could remind him that he was to wait for her after they arrived at Sella di Corno. She told him she would be immediately returning to the buggy to leave Sella for another destination. He had received a portion of the extra money her father had given her, so he had agreed to extend the trip. "*Si, signora,*" he had said. "*Capisco*" (I understand).

She settled back as he resumed the journey. Although every cell of her body wept, her eyes were dry. Her thoughts roamed chaotically from Vasto to Sella di Corno: to the harsh sound of the buggy wheels on the rough road, then back to Vasto with flashes of sea and family faces, back to Sella where she sought to black out any specific faces and back to the buggy wheels on the road. She felt her mind would snap when a sharp turn in the road abruptly brought her attention back to the present. They had entered Sella di Corno. The village was completely still. She directed the driver to the local police station, awakened the children, gathered up their bags, and stepped down from the buggy. An inner paralysis cut off all her feelings. She moved like an automaton. As she walked toward the entrance, she looked back and reminded the driver to wait.

Seated at a desk littered with papers, the lone officer on duty was nodding off drowsily. The candle had burned down to where it gave a small range of light. Next to the desk was a chair and across the small room, benches were set against the wall. He was startled when he heard footsteps and a woman's voice say, "*Buona sera*" (good evening). In the dim light, he saw a woman with three small children.

Before he could return her "*Buona sera,*" she spoke again. "We are the Ferrara family, Francesco Ferrara. These are his children. Would you be so kind as to let them sit here while I go back and pay the driver?" she asked.

"Of course, *signora,*" he answered. He helped settle the sleepy children on the benches and piled up their bags next to them.

Without another word, without another look back, she walked out of the door, climbed into the carriage and out of her children's lives. . . forever.

Chapter Five

On the day Maria was to arrive, Francesco kept himself busy to keep his excitement under control. As evening blended into the night, he became concerned. They should have arrived by now. They were expected that afternoon. His thoughts turned to Maria—he had missed her terribly—her sweet voice—her warm body next to his—her gentle touch. He had missed the children—Maddalena with her quiet but sometimes mischievous nature; Cristoforo and Michele who still hung on Maria like appendages. He wished he had not let them go. It had been too long of an absence.

Lost in his thoughts, he barely heard the knock on the door. When he did, his heart leapt with joy. They were here! At last he would embrace her and feel the tug of the children's arms around his legs. In his excitement and rush to get to the door, he knocked over a chair which woke up his father Cristoforo and step-mother Amelia. Francesco threw open the door in wild anticipation. When he saw a policeman with his three children, he was stunned into silence while his mind screamed, "She's dead! She's dead! Maria is dead! Oh, my God!"

When he regained his voice, he cried out in agony, "Where is Maria?"

The crying children rushed to him and the policeman stepped into the room. Francesco briefly tried to comfort them, and then ushered them to their grandfather Cristoforo. He grabbed the policeman's shirt and shook him. With a fear crazed voice, he yelled, "Speak! Speak! Speak! For God's sake."

The policeman, firmly but kindly, removed the clutching hands and said, "Calm down, Francesco. She is not dead."

"Then where is she?" Francesco's relieved but choked voice asked.

The policeman recounted the story that after Maria left the children, she said she had to go back and pay the driver, but then she did not come back. He had waited awhile, then went out to look for her. The buggy was gone. There was no one in sight.

"After a time," he added, "I realized that she was not coming back. The children were cold and frightened and I thought it best to bring them home. That's all I can tell you. Now I must go. Tomorrow we can talk again."

Cristoforo showed the policeman to the door and when he returned he found Francesco frantically pacing the floor. His face filled with anguish and fear, he turned to his father. He could hardly choke out the words. "I must go find her. She may have been kidnapped. They may even have killed her. Help me get the horse ready so I can leave at once."

As he prepared to leave, his mind whirled, tumbling from one idea to another. Why did she say she had to pay the driver? He had already been paid. What would make her say that? It didn't make sense. She was here—she had arrived safely. Why had she not come directly home? Suddenly, the whirling stopped. His blood drained out of him and a cold chill shook him. Could she? Would she? No! It was too horrible to even think of it. He knew she loved the children—there was no doubt of that. Yet, she had clearly shown him that she suffered terribly from the caravan, the villagers, Amelia, and even his criticism. So, she was always trying to get back to Vasto and delaying coming back home. Now it was clear to him. She had abandoned the children. The blood surged back into his body in an explosive rush. The cold chill turned into hot, overpowering rage.

He rushed out of the house and met his father at the foot of the narrow stairway. As he mounted his horse, he roared, "I'm going after her. She can't have gotten too far."

A crushed Cristoforo could only say to his son, *"Addio."*

As Francesco sped away into the night, he began to develop his plan. He would track Maria down at the inns where she and the children had stayed. She would have to stop somewhere to rest. If she somehow got back to Vasto, he would go there and bring her back, he would never let her go again.

By the next evening, he reached the last inn. No one had seen her since she had been there with the children. Exhausted, yet propelled by his rage, he set out for Vasto. Doubts began to assail him—was he wrong in thinking that she had abandoned the children? Could the driver have robbed her and done away with her? But he knew the driver and trusted him. Besides she did not carry extra money. And why would she say she had to go back and pay the driver? Yes. She had abandoned both him and the children. The horrible thought tormented him.

Morning broke over the countryside as he approached the outskirts of Vasto. He had always enjoyed the village with its unique position overlooking the sea. The cool morning breeze fell gently on his face and seemed to soothe the effects of the hard ride, if only for a moment. As he approached the Ianieri family home, he tried to compose his thoughts. Before he could form the words, he was at the front door. A sleepy Luigi greeted him and instantly became fully awake. He could hardly believe his eyes and could find no words when Francesco asked, "Where is she?"

When Luigi was finally able to speak he said, "Francesco, what are you doing here—and where is who?"

Impatiently, Francesco answered, "Maria—where is she?"

Unable to comprehend the situation, Luigi said, "She's with you. She left some days ago. Didn't she arrive yet?"

Francesco now knew the bitter truth and explained everything to Luigi. The unbelieving Luigi thought back to the days before her departure, and he remembered the intense protestations she had made about going back. It was clear to him as well.

But still, where was she? Where had she gone? Was she hiding somewhere in Vasto? In a town nearby? No—everyone knew everything about everybody; she would never be able to stay hidden here.

"Where shall I look for her?" asked Francesco in a weary voice.

"Come," Luigi touched his shoulder, "you are exhausted and need some food and drink. We will talk about it some more after you have rested."

There was little more to say. That afternoon, Francesco started back to Sella di Corno. The unanswered questions would have to wait.

That same afternoon, the village of Vasto was in an uproar. Word had spread like wildfire and the fountain talk buzzed about all the possibilities of why she did it, how she did it, and where she might be. Only the Ianieris sat behind closed doors suffering from the worst *disgrazia* that could befall an Italian family. Months later people would draw their own conclusions about what had happened. Some said that Francesco had killed her. Others claimed that she was seen boarding a ship in Naples for America. Whatever had happened, Maria was never seen again.

Chapter Six

Maria's disappearance cast a pall over all the members of the household. After the first several weeks of stunned silence, Maddalena approached her father. "Babbo," she asked, "when is Mamma coming home?"

Francesco looked startled, as if she had awakened him from a deep sleep. "I don't know," he answered flatly.

Maddalena continued, "But, Babbo, where is she?"

Again Francesco barely got the words out, "I don't know."

Maddalena persisted, and asked, "Why did she leave?"

Francesco, in a stern, cold, irritated voice, which was meant to shut the door on her questioning, answered sharply and emphatically, "Maddalena, *acqua in bocca*," (water in the mouth), meaning she was not to talk about it.

Drawing back as if to ward off a blow, tears brimming in her eyes, her tortured voice uncontrollably whispered the words, "I miss her."

But Francesco had already turned and walked away. He could not bear talking about it, although somehow he saw Maria everywhere. As he traveled to many towns and villages to get contracts for the charcoal, she was his constant companion. He ranted at her. He raged at her. Then he crumbled under the memory of her beauty, her softness, and her gentle nature. Guilt overcame him as he recalled the harshness of the work imposed on her, the rejection of her by the villagers, and finally his inability to change or control things.

It was especially difficult when he went to Vasto and suffered the

Ianieri family's scorn and the townspeople's gossip about whether Maria had met her death at the hands of a killer or had managed to leave for America out of Naples.

He knew his children suffered under Amelia's cold harshness, but again, he had no control. The only way he could cope with the emotional turmoil of his children, bereft of their mother and unloved by their step-grandmother, was to ignore their questions and remove himself from the situation by throwing himself into his business travels.

Maddalena never asked again. It was not allowed. She created in herself a secret place where the ache and the longing lodged itself. She had lived on expectations, and now they were shattered.

Months later she would try to remember her mother's face, but all she could bring back was her presence—the voice that felt like a gentle caress, the warmth that surrounded her like a cozy blanket, the sense of playfulness that had brought joy to her heart.

In the midst of this chaos, Maddalena withdrew into a tiny circle of fear and pain, saying nothing and asking for nothing. Only to the little Cristoforo did she sometimes whisper, "Don't worry. Mamma is coming back." The spirit in her soft, brown eyes dimmed and a grief-stricken veil overshadowed the rest of her life. Cristoforo, on the other hand, kept running off all hours of the day and night. When he would be finally discovered in some corner of the village wandering about desolately, his response was always the same. "I'm looking for my Mamma." His five-year-old mind refused to believe that she was not somewhere close by and he would find her. After many months, Cristoforo stopped running away to hunt for his mother. His world lost its shine and became a dull gray. Michele, too young to understand, whined a little at first, and then fell into the routine of the situation. His grandfather Cristoforo was heart-broken. Amelia's constant grim, tight lips revealed her white-hot anger.

Cristoforo began tugging at Maddelena's skirt to go to the piazza. She turned to Nonna Amelia for permission. "*Va, va*" (go, go), Amelia answered impatiently. Amelia was always eager to get the children out of the house. The long cold winters that kept them indoors drove her crazy. She watched as Maddalena took Cristoforo's hand and walked out the door. Her hatred for their mother surged within her. Maria's disappearance cast an unwanted burden on her. Now responsible for the children, she felt trapped with no recourse. But she would teach them what the world was like.

Amelia herself had found out how harsh the world could be when she left her own village to marry Nonno Cristoforo and move to Sella di Corno. She had longed to have a husband and family but didn't want to leave her village. Her family had made that decision for her. The prosperous, kindly Cristoforo overcame her doubts. In his own village, he was considered a real catch. His first wife had died, and each eligible woman in the village secretly dreamed that she would be the one he would choose to marry. He was a large man, although short of stature, and he had an expansive smile and a benevolent manner. His charcoal business was the only other business in the village—other than the Chiuppi store. Not only was he highly respected, but he was also well-liked. When he had returned from a business trip with a new wife, the women of the village reacted with shock and anger.

"Why not one of us?" they muttered to each other.

"Look, she's all skin and bones, and she has cold eyes," one snickered.

"Who does she think she is? A stranger, but she thinks she's superior to all of us," said Concetta. This put the final stamp of disapproval on the situation and sealed Amelia's status as a village outsider.

Amelia had been chilled by the rejection of the village women. She had not expected to be welcomed with open arms, given that many of them hoped for a chance to marry this successful, kind man. However, she had not expected the icy reception she got the first time she went for water at the well in the piazza. No one had spoken to her—the only recognition she received was a nod of the head or a shrug of the shoulders in her direction.

Amelia seethed with anger at the memory. She didn't deserve this, and she vowed every one of them would pay, starting with these unwanted children that had been dumped upon her. Except for Michele, who brought a fragile vulnerability that somehow broke through her own pain,when he arrived at three years of age. Happy to have gotten rid of the two older children for a while, she watched as he played quietly with his toys.

Chapter Seven

On the outskirts of the village, set in a clump of trees on higher ground was the Mound—a small hill where the sheepherders brought their sheep each morning and released them to freely graze the mountainsides. At the end of a day's labor, the men returned to call them back to their stalls. The Mound looked down across a broad valley that resembled a gigantic patchwork quilt of vegetation. The colors of soft green, warm gold, and velvety brown all indicated wheat fields in different stages of growth. Surrounding this valley were deep green wooded foothills. Above the encircling foothills, towering above the valley, were the Abruzzo peaks—barren, jagged outlines of the Apennines with the Gran Sasso (big stone), the highest point of the Apennine Range, reigning over all.

On this Mound, under a leafy tree, sat Maddalena, now thirteen, and Cristoforo, eleven, munching on chunks of bread. Six years had passed since their mother abandoned them. Maddalena broke a piece off the large loaf lying in her lap and gave it to Cristoforo. "Don't eat too fast," she warned, "it will make you sick." Cristoforo grabbed the chunk and hungrily chewed it, ignoring his sister's caution. "You know," Maddalena continued, "Nonna (Amelia) would be very angry if she knew we took this loaf of bread. What we don't finish we will feed to the birds."

"Yes, I remember when she punished you for breaking off just one piece," Cristoforo added sadly. "But why does Nonna say we must go hungry so we can understand what hunger is?"

"I don't know," Maddalena answered, "but don't you worry. Now

I know how to take a whole loaf, hide it in my skirt, and come here where we can eat. Then we won't have to be hungry. She will not miss it because there are so many loaves."

They had managed to support each other the past six years to overcome the persistent negativity of Nonna Amelia and the lack of their father's attention which, when he was traveling, was nonexistent and when at home, erratic. Sometimes when he looked at his children, the pain overcame him and he withdrew from them. Only Nonno Cristoforo dropped crumbs of warmth over them.

Cristoforo blissfully savored the bread as he looked up with affection at the sister who always managed to find a way to comfort him. The bond forged now would last the rest of their lives.

Maddalena awoke to a disturbing sensation. She felt a warm, wet substance between her thighs. She jumped up out of bed and saw a red stain on the sheets. It was also on her nightgown. The substance began to flow out of her, and she realized that it was blood. Without thinking, she called out, "Babbo, Babbo," but her father was out of town, and her cries brought Amelia from the kitchen, where she had been preparing breakfast.

"Nonna," she cried, her voice trembling with fear, "I'm bleeding. I'm dying. What is wrong with me?"

For a moment, Amelia's heart softened, remembering her own fearful, lonely discovery. Quickly, however, she pushed away the thought and spoke in her usual tight, angry words. "It's nothing. Now you're a lady. Come, I'll give you a rag to cover it."

The words did not calm Maddalena's fear. What did she mean 'a lady'? Why did blood make you 'a lady'? She only knew losing blood could mean death.

"Come, come," Amelia brusquely directed her out of the bedroom where her two brothers lay awakened by the cries, but remained quietly in their beds.

"Come into the kitchen," Amelia directed her.

Maddalena was afraid to walk, for fear it would all gush out of her and she would fall dead. Amelia's reassurances did not relieve her terror.

But obediently she walked stiffly into the kitchen, where Amelia already was tearing an old sheet into strips and then forming the strips into a pad. Handing the cloth and two pins to the shaking girl, she said, "Here, put this rag over it and pin it to your panties. Tomorrow I will give you a new one and you can wash the old one out to reuse the next day."

Her matter-of-fact tone began to calm Maddalena's fears. It must be something that's happened before, she thought. But what does it mean? Why blood? As she covered the bleeding place and pinned the rag to her panties, she gave up trying to understand. She would be too embarrassed to ask Nonno or her father. Months later, when the blood had come back regularly, she became used to it and lost her fear.

It was only in the piazza when she tentatively questioned the storekeeper's daughter, Anna Felice, who was a year older, that she found out it meant she could have babies. Anna Felice had an older sister, Bettina, who was married and had children. It was Bettina who had given her sister the explanation that the midwife had given her when she had her first baby. "The blood is necessary to feed the unborn, and if you are not having a baby, it just comes out."

Maddalena was stunned. So that's what being 'a lady' meant.

Chapter Eight

The piazza was abuzz with excitement. Massimo Chiuppi had returned from Aquila once again. The first time, following his apprenticeship to a well-known tailor, he had been hired to measure women for corsets and to make alterations for men and women's clothing. Customers soon complained about his surly nature and, after losing some of his best clientele, the master tailor fired him. Massimo then returned home to help in the family store, which he hated and soon took it out on everyone around him.

Three years later his family made another attempt to send him to Aquila, where, being a larger town, there were more possibilities for using his tailoring knowledge to make a living. Once again, he lost customers and found no other source of work. So he returned to Sella. The piazza gossip began again.

"He's worse than ever," Concetta mused, "and I hear he was his usually nasty self in Aquila."

"He'll never change," ventured Gina, "a man who raises his hand to his mother and flies into rages over nothing is impossible to have around."

"Remember," chimed in Luisa, "when he made a shambles of the store over nothing. His mother and father were so embarrassed that they closed the store for two days to put things together again."

"I swear he has a devil inside him," Concetta offered, "he has such good parents. They don't deserve being so badly treated by their first-born son."

"And now Giulio is beginning to follow in his brother's footsteps. He's such a rascal, and always in trouble," added Luisa.

Following the revelation from Nonna Amelia about "becoming a lady," Maddalena felt different. At times she felt moody and at other times excited. She couldn't understand the ups and downs of her feelings. As usual, she turned to Anna Felice who seemed to know everything and was more than willing to supply answers.

"Oh," she answered Maddalena's question, "that's all normal. My big sister Bettina told me she felt like that too, when I asked her about it."

"Really?" Maddalena replied. "But why?"

"I don't know, except that Bettina said we would want to start having babies, and she must be right because she already has three of them," asserted Anna Felice proudly.

"But how did she get the babies?" Maddalena persisted.

At that point, Anna Felice drew Maddalena away from the others and whispered into her ear the desired information. Maddalena shrank back in horror!

"Oh, no!" she cried. "Oh, no! Not Mamma and Babbo! Not Nonna and Nonno!" She felt panicked. A great fear came over here. "It's not true—it can't be true!"

"It *is* true," countered Anna Felice, "my sister Bettina doesn't lie. Besides, it happened to her when she married Tomasso, and they started having the babies right away because of it."

Maddalena wanted to hear no more. She turned away and quickly left the piazza to go sit on the Mound. There she could sort out the feelings and emotions that had swept over her. Could that happen to her? Could they make her marry, and she too would have to do "it" so she could have babies? It was too horrible to think about. She set it aside and walked back home, shuddering as she passed the grocery store, not daring to look to see who was behind the counter.

The Mound had been the special refuge for Maddalena and Cristoforo. She had begun to take Felicetta and Assunta there instead of going to the piazza so they could avoid the prying eyes and ears of Anna Felice. Here they were able to share their thoughts and feelings in private. It was so delicious sitting under the trees, letting the quiet surround them, speaking in intimate whispers about the changes in their bodies and their new interest in boys.

"I think Paolo was looking at me in the piazza yesterday. Do you think he's handsome, Maddalena?" Felicetta asked.

Intercepting the answer, Assunta quickly said, "Not as handsome as his brother, Bennie. What do you think, Maddalena?"

Caught between the sisters' rivalry for the best looking of the two brothers, Maddalena hesitated, "Well, I don't know. They're different, but I think they're both handsome," she responded.

Satisfied, the two sisters hugged their knees, looked down on the sprawling valley below, and fell into a quiet state of dreamy thoughts about their romantic futures. No one spoke. A light breeze ruffled the leaves in the trees around them. In the distance, the call of a sheepherder broke the silence and Assunta jumped up.

"Let's go," she urged, "they might be in the piazza right now."

"Wait," said Felicetta, turning to Maddalena she asked, "how about you, Maddalena? Is there anyone you like?"

Maddalena was taken aback—she had never even thought about it. She felt uneasy about these things. She stammered, "I—I—I don't know."

"Oh well, let's go." said Assunta, impatient to move on.

"Keep your eyes open, Maddalena. Look around and see if you like someone."

As they entered the piazza, Anna Felice came rushing toward them. Her face was flushed and she looked angry. "Oh! There you are," she called out, her voice harsh and cold.

They drew back and Assunta asked, "What's wrong?"

Pulling them aside, Anna Felice broke the news. "How could they do this to me? How could they do this to me? I won't do it! They can kill me. I won't do it! I'll run away. I won't do it!"

Assunta finally interrupted, "Do what? What do they want you to do?"

The three girls looked at each other, mystified and waited for the next outburst. Instead, lowering her voice, Anna Felice spit out the words through gritted teeth, "They said I am to marry Attilio."

"Attilio?" gasped Assunta. "He's so old and a widower for many years."

"That's what I mean," hissed Anna Felice, "I begged my father and mother to let me wait a little longer before they marry me off, but, oh no, their minds are made up."

Gently and sympathetically, Felicetta tried to calm her down, asking, "Can't Massimo, your brother, talk to them and help you out? Or maybe Bettina?"

With a contorted face and a raspy voice that crackled with hate, Anna Felice almost spat out the words, "I hate my brother! He only cares about himself, first, last, and always. He gives my parents so much trouble, we all wish he would go away forever. And poor Bettina has more babies than she can take care of. No, I'm stuck … and the worst of it is that he is taking me to America right after we're married. Who wants to go to a strange country? I like it here in Sella di Corno. I don't want to go anywhere else. How could my parents do this to me?"

"America," Felicetta broke in, "that's where Paolo and Bennie always talk about going some day. They say it's easy to get rich in America, and everybody is happy."

"Well, let them go!" sputtered Anna Felice. "I want to stay right here. I hate America. I hate Attilio and I hate my parents too!"

Her fury held the girls in a suspended, cold silence during which they tried to absorb the bad news. The chatter of the women around the fountain and the screams of the playing children brought them back into focus.

"Attilio," thought Maddalena, "that old man, always staring at the young girls!" It made her shudder, and at the same time feel grateful that she was not the sacrificial lamb. Yet she wondered what the future held for her. She felt a sharp pang of fear and a gnawing anxiety. She marveled that Felicetta and Assunta could be so excited and joyful about their feelings for the Mangini brothers, as if they were sure that eventually they would be married to them.

Felicetta, having spotted Paolo at the other end of the piazza, whispered, "Look, there he is, over by the bar."

"What? Where?" asked Assunta, "Is Bennie there too?"

"I don't know," answered Felicetta.

"Let's walk around and get closer," Assunta suggested.

"I don't want to," huffed Anna Felice, miffed that they so easily shrugged off the terrible dilemma of her life. Grabbing Maddalena by the arm, she turned away from the two sisters and walked in the opposite direction.

In spite of her protestations, within several weeks, the banns were announced in church of the forthcoming marriage of Anna Felice Chiuppi and Attilio Santori. Shortly after the marriage, they left for America. Through it all, Anna Felice maintained a cold, angry look that only Attilio mistook as the reticence and natural fear of a young girl.

When the excitement over the wedding and the departure of the couple died down, Felicetta and Assunta could do nothing but talk about Paolo and Bennie. The boys' family were sheepherders, highly respected in the village. Paolo was a year older than Bennie, and the brothers were inseparable. Paolo was the more dominant of the two, and the young people in the village looked to him for leadership. Bennie adored his brother and was satisfied to follow in his footsteps. When Paolo spoke of his determination to go to America, Bennie added his intention to go with him. They talked about their attraction to the two sisters, Felicetta and Assunta.

"Felicetta is sweet and kind," shared Paolo.

"Yeah, she is, but I like Assunta better. Felicetta is quiet and serious but Assunta is lively and full of fun. Do you think they like us, Paolo?" he asked.

"I think so," answered Paolo, "why don't we ask them to walk around the piazza with us. We can talk and maybe buy them a gelato. We'll be able to tell by the way they act and see if they try to get away from us. If we do that a lot, and they like it, I think we'll have our answer."

"Good idea. I know that Assunta is the one for me. No other girl in the village has her sparkle. I really hope she likes me," sighed Bennie. The courtship began and, after many gelatos, the two pairs became accepted couples in the piazza.

In the ensuing days, the girls met on the Mound. Assunta glowed. "Oh my God!" she kept repeating as she danced around the Mound, prancing and pirouetting, almost beside herself with joy.

"Oh, my God! He really likes me. I know he really likes me. Last Friday during our walk, when he handed me my gelato, he kept his hand on mine as long as he could and looked right into my eyes. I felt like he wanted to eat me up instead of his gelato. Oh my God! I'm so happy!" The words came tumbling out one after the other like her dancing feet on the Mound.

Felicetta and Maddalena smiled at each other, smiled at Assunta, and they all reveled in her joy. Finally, settling herself on the ground, Assunta went on, "Now, Felicetta, you looked pretty happy. How is it with you and Paolo?"

In her quiet, understated way, Felicetta answered, "We have promised each other to each other."

Felicetta's words set Assunta off again. Unable to contain herself, she was back on her feet, flying from Felicetta to Maddalena, back and forth, hugging them, hugging herself, throwing her arms up to the sky as if to hug the whole world.

Soon the village was full of talk about the possibility of a double wedding. Both families were well-liked, and after experiencing the sour marriage of Anna Felice and Attilio, the women at the well vicariously exulted in the fulfillment of young love. Once again, the banns were posted, but this time, everyone in the village joined in preparing for the happy event. The only sad part was the boys' plan to go to America to a city called Chicago. Though they wished them well, they would miss the four young people who added so much life to the village.

After the double wedding, the two couples began making preparations to leave, and a shadow fell over the village. Maddalena ached with despair. She would be alone. Of course, Cristoforo would always be there, but no one could replace the love and warmth of her friendship with Felicetta and Assunta. She tried to look happy during the festivities, but her heart was heavy. On the day they left, she felt as if her insides had been torn out of her. She could not find her voice to say good-bye. She could only go to the Mound and weep.

Chapter Nine

Maddalena heard them whispering in the night. They hardly ever did that, and somehow she felt they were talking about her. Occasionally her father's voice rose above the others with an emphatic "No!" She worried. Were they going to send her away? Then she heard Nonno's placating voice, and everything became quiet again. She nestled back under the covers and gave in to her fatigue.

Maddalena worked very hard to please Amelia and avoid her wrath. She had grown taller. She had thick black hair and luminous brown eyes, which remained guarded at home but came to life in the piazza as she gave in to her playful nature. She felt a pride in her changing body as her breasts matured and her hips filled out. She noticed the other girls in the piazza who also were her age. "Now I'm a <u>lady</u>," she thought as she recalled Amelia's comment—yet the pride was mixed with a deep fear: what was next? What was going to happen to her? Anna Felice's words haunted her. Now she could make babies! What did that mean for her?

The next day she asked Cristoforo if he had heard what they talked about, for he slept closer to their father's room. Cristoforo, now thirteen years old, was considered grown-up enough to help in the caravan and with all the heavier duties around the house. His body was thin and wiry, and he had a constant look of hunger in his eyes. He looked at his sister and wondered how her maturing would impact him. He depended on her for the only warmth in his life. He knew she would always answer his questions honestly, and, when he needed comfort and reassurance, she never failed him. He adored her and feared that, if she left, he would truly be alone. They had decided not to apprentice him to learn a trade since he could work in the family business, and at seventeen would enter the army for his required two years of service. He felt his future was already mapped out, but what about Maddalena's? What would happen to her? He knew that marriage was next for her, but what if she had to go to another village? What would he do? How could he live without her? Up to now, she had filled the cold, deep hole in his heart.

She persisted. "Well? Did you hear what they were whispering about?"

"Maddalena," he answered, "you know how tired I am at the end of the day. I'm gone the minute my head hits the pillow. I'm sorry, but I heard nothing."

"*Va bene*" (it's ok). She tousled his hair, tenderly. "It's probably nothing. But you work too hard with not enough to eat. I talked to Babbo about it, and he does not believe me. So we will continue to steal the bread and go to the Mound," she assured him.

Their love for each other poured out as they smiled and then went to perform their daily duties.

One month later Maddalena returned from the piazza to find Massimo visiting her family. As she opened the door and saw him talking to them, fear overcame her, and she fled to the Mound. Her stomach in knots and her heart pounding, she asked herself, "What does it mean? He has never been in our house before. Could it have something to do with me?"

She felt she was going to burst. She needed to talk to someone. Who could she turn to? Felicetta and Assunta were gone. Cristoforo was away in the mountains. She felt trapped. Babbo was a possibility, but he always stopped her questioning with "*acqua in bocca.*" Her only resource might be Nonno. His basic goodness and kindness was held back by Amelia's iron control, but, at times, he gave his grandchildren the only solace they received in the cold detached family. No, she could not talk to anyone. She would have to wait and see what happened next.

The more she thought about it, the more she began to feel foolish. "How silly of me," she laughed. "It has nothing to do with me at all. They are probably making some business deals."

A wave of relief came over her. She got up, shook off the leaves that had fallen on her skirt and stood gazing at the village with its red tiled roofs. Beyond were the distant valleys that lay verdant and pregnant with the emerging wheat. A burst of poignancy flooded her body at the beauty before her. She missed Felicetta and Assunta. Reluctantly, she left the Mound to slowly wend her way home.

The next few days flowed uneventfully, filled with the usual daily routine. Cristoforo was back from the caravan. Michele, at ten years of age, was getting stronger and taking part in the lighter business activities, one of which included the care of the mules. Because of the bitterly cold mountain winters, it was necessary to provide a warm space at night for the animals on the first floor of their three-storied home. During the day the mules were let out to feed. It was Michele's duty to bring them in at night. The mules were the backbone of the caravan activities.

Michele was slight and tended to illness. It was difficult for him to run up and down the lengthy staircase that led from their third-floor dwelling to the mules on the first floor. When fatigue overcame him, he would forego the journey to the piazza. In this way he spent more time at home with his step-grandmother and grandfather.

The peaceful routine was soon interrupted by another visit from Massimo. Maddalena was home at the time. She noticed that since he had started his visits, the whispering at night had stopped. Cristoforo had never been able to stay awake long enough to catch any of the conversations. As soon as Massimo had settled himself, Nonno brought out a bottle of wine. In the process, Maddalena made her escape—hurrying to the door as fast as she could, her heart pounding as if it would break out of her body.

"Maddalena," she heard Nonno call out.

But she was already gone before he could utter another word. She flew down the three flights of stairs and hurried to the piazza. There she sat in a corner, watching the women and children at the fountain. She had no desire to join them, her playful spirit dampened for the moment. Besides, for her, the piazza was bereft of her best friends, and she wanted no others.

After enough time had passed, and she knew that Massimo would be gone, Maddalena slowly walked back, slowly climbed the stairway and entered her home. Nonno greeted her. When she tried to go right to her bedroom, he stopped her and asked, "Why did you run away so fast? When I called to you, you were already gone."

Mutely, she stood staring at the floor, wishing she could ask him the fearful question in her heart.

"Go, go," he said gently, "your grandmother needs your help."

With the *acqua in bocca* engrained into her, Maddalena could not find her voice and, saying nothing, moved toward the kitchen.

The next morning started out as an ordinary July day. Michele had led the mules out to graze, and Cristoforo was stacking the charcoal. Maddalena had prepared breakfast for the family, one of her new duties since her recent fifteenth birthday. It was 1908. The weather promised an easy summer day. Maddalena was eager to flee to the Mound, but Nonna Amelia stopped her.

"Wait," she said. "Don't be so fast to run away all the time. I have something to tell you. Sit down." They were in the kitchen, and Nonna Amelia had just taken off her apron. Placing it on the back of the chair, she sat opposite Maddalena. "You know, you are now of marriageable age," she began in her cold, irritated voice.

Maddalena's heart sank. She felt an internal scream shaping up inside of her. She wanted to break up into a thousand little pieces, to be tossed into the open sky, and carried away, never to be seen again. From an enormous distance, she heard the voice tattooing the words onto her, "Grandfather and Massimo have agreed to a dowry. You are to marry Massimo as soon as the banns are posted. You are a lucky girl to have a business man for a husband."

The whisperings in the night, the visits from Massimo—the awful truth blinded her. It galvanized her. She leaped to her feet. Barely able to see, she fled down the stairway. Holding back her tears and rage, she raced through the town to the Mound. Once there, with one explosion of breath, she threw herself on the ground under the tree where she and Cristoforo often had sought refuge. Her body convulsed as an avalanche of tears poured out of her onto the dry leaves.

Horror and fear flooded her body and soul. She lay face down and shook and wept. Then she lay face up and shook and wept some more. When it seemed like hours had passed, when no more tears would come and her body's shaking was spent, she gave herself up to the soft earth beneath her.

Then she thought of her mother. How she longed for her. She dimly remembered her sweetness, her softness. But hard as she tried, she could not bring back her face. The ache that had lain dormant all these years now burst into life. She longed for her mother.

Memories of Vasto began to flood over her—the blue sea, the warm sand, the laughter of her cousins, the gentleness of Giuseppina, her nurse. Now it became clear to her. Now she knew what to do. She would run away to Vasto. She began to plan how, when she realized she had only the clothes she was wearing. She could not go home—no!—she would never go back. She would start walking and would ask people the way. She would wait for nightfall so that the darkness could hide her.

Her thoughts were interrupted by Cristoforo's voice. "Maddalena, why haven't you come home? It's dinner time already, and everyone is wondering where you are."

Pulling Cristoforo down to her, she pleaded, "Oh, please, please, Cristoforo. Don't tell them where I am. Please. Help me. I can never go back—never—you must help me!"

"Don't be silly, Maddalena," he began. But when he saw her anguish, he paused and then asked, "What's wrong? What has happened? You know, we are older now. Nonna Amelia can't hurt us anymore. We can take care of ourselves." he reassured her.

"But you don't know," she answered, "you don't know!"

He looked at her tear-stained face. He had never seen her so distraught. It frightened him. "Don't know what, Maddalena? Don't know what? Tell me!"

He threw his arms around her. She was cold and shaking. The July warmth had receded before the night's cold mountain air. Barely forming the words, she wailed in broken cries, "They—they...."

"Who are they? Tell me!" Cristoforo urged.

"Massimo, Massimo!" Again she choked on the words.

Standing up, Cristoforo looked down at her protectively and demanded that she reveal the rest. "Has Massimo been treating you badly again? You know it's not only you—it's everyone. You shouldn't let it bother you."

For the moment he felt relieved. This was an old story, and she was simply taking it too hard. "Come," he pulled at her to get up, "let's go home, it's getting cold, and soon it will be dark."

Terrified, Maddalena tore away from him. "You don't understand!" she screamed. "You don't understand!"

Now he was really frightened by her extreme hysteria, as she continued to scream, "I'm going to run away. I'm never going home!"

Her terror brought out his strength, and again he took her into his arms to quiet and comfort her. "Don't worry, Maddalena. I'll help you." He stroked her head, patted her back, and rocked her gently in his arms. Feeling the protection and love of her brother's arms around her, she told Cristoforo the awful truth. "They are making me marry <u>him.</u>"

Stunned, he moved back from her as if the force of a great wind had blown him over. "No! Never!" he bellowed. He drew himself up to his thirteen-year-old height and declared, "I won't let them."

"What can <u>you</u> do?" she countered. "Please help me run away!"

He sat down under the tree and drew her next to him. Rage began to well up in him, followed by anguish. How could he help her in this awful moment? What could he do for her? She, who had consoled him. She, who had comforted him, who had warmed his heart and protected him. Now that she needed <u>him</u>, what could he do for <u>her</u>?

They sat together, his arm holding her close to him. "We'll run away together," he said in as strong a voice as he could muster. He felt her shiver with the cold, and he realized the hopelessness of it. If they did not return, everyone in the village would turn out to look for them. If they took to walking all the roads, they would be discovered very quickly. If they went into the mountains, there were no paths. The darkness was impenetrable. The danger of mountain animals was very real. He understood that there was no way out of the situation—unless he could convince Nonno to save her.

With resolve in his voice, he said, "Maddalena, listen. If we run away, they will find us. Our only hope is to get Nonno to understand and to cancel the agreement. I will go home and talk to him. When I come back, I'll bring a jacket and a sandwich for you. Wait for me— then we will decide what to do."

She looked up at him adoringly—and a bit skeptically, and replied, "Oh, Cristoforo, I knew you would help me. Please hurry back."

By this time it was darker and even colder. She had never before been on the Mound so late into the night. The familiar cries of the sheepherders earlier had brought her comfort, but now all was silent and new fears came over her. She shut them out as she dreamed of Vasto and a new life of love and warmth and kindness.

It seemed like hours later when she heard footsteps and then Cristoforo's voice, calling out to her as he approached. When she looked up, she saw him—her jacket in one hand, a sandwich in the other, and next to him. . . .Nonno. Looking at her grandfather, Maddalena instinctively knew the futility of it all. Cristoforo helped her into her jacket. She declined the sandwich. Spent, she quietly followed them home.

Two weeks later, the banns of the wedding of Massimo Chiuppi and Maddalena Ferrara were announced at Sunday Mass. It is the custom of the Catholic Church that prospective marriages are presented to the community publicly at the Sunday Mass for three consecutive weeks. This gives any member of the community an opportunity to speak out against the marriage. If no one complains, the ceremony is allowed to proceed. The social life of Sella di Corno was centered around the piazza and the church activities. Sunday Mass was the high point of the week. Everyone wore their best clothes and usually gathered after the service in the church hall, or if the weather permitted, in the church garden.

This particular Sunday—the day the banns were first read—was a lovely July morning. Everyone milled around outside after the Mass was over. When they could, the women pulled each other aside for a quick comment on the shocking news.

"Well! She finally did it! Amelia could hardly wait till she pushed the poor girl out the door," said Concetta with an acid tone in her voice.

"It's so unfair. Such a sweet, innocent child!" added Chiarina.

"A lamb to slaughter," sadly commented Luisa.

They shook their heads and quickly returned to their families. It was time to head home and prepare the main meal of the day, the Sunday *pranzo* (lunch).

It would be later that evening during the *passeggiata* (the walk) in the piazza that they would give rein to the anger and sadness they felt. Their anger at Amelia spilled over to Francesco.

"How could a father allow this to happen to his daughter?"

"And why doesn't her grandfather Cristoforo, the head of the household, put his foot down and stop it?"

"Who can deal with Amelia? She will make their lives miserable if she doesn't get her way."

The comments spilled out, one on top of the other.

The piazza was filled with young people, but Maddalena was not among them. She had not appeared since the day Amelia had dropped her bomb.

"I hear she stopped eating," ventured Chiarina.

"It's no wonder," sighed Luisa, "who could stomach the thought of a life with a man like him!"

"After losing her mother and then living with such a step-grandmother, the girl doesn't deserve such a cruel fate," bemoaned Concetta.

As the evening wore on, everyone gradually moved on and left for home.

The courtship was over, and years later Massimo would laughingly recount how Maddalena turned her back and ran from him when he went to her house—"All I ever saw of her was her ass!"

The wedding took place in August of 1909. Maddalena, at fifteen years of age, was forced into a marriage from which there was no exit.

Chapter Ten

After they were married, he showered her with indignities. Fear and despair numbed her body and soul. She had gone through the ceremony like an automaton—pushing the thought of her wedding night into some far off place or she would have succumbed to her other thought of killing herself.

The women in the piazza looked for her the next day. Maddalena did not show up. Each day they murmured to each other, "*Poverina* (poor little one), can you imagine a brute like him with that fifteen year old child and he twenty-nine?" Their voices stilled as each one visualized their own version of the horrible experience.

"God give her strength," prayed Chiarina, as they gathered up their *concas*, balancing them on their heads and with graceful, firm stances headed for home.

A week later, they held their breath—"Here she comes," whispered Luisa. They dispersed and finally Concetta greeted her... "*Buon giorno*, Maddalena. "*Come va?*" (How's it going?)

With eyes cast down, Maddalena very quietly answered, "*Bene, grazie.*" Hurriedly she filled her *conca* and left immediately. As her figure disappeared from the piazza, they gathered to share their feelings.

"Did you see those sunken eyes filled with sadness?" said Concetta.

"Not to mention the big dark circles underneath them. What a cross to put on that child's shoulders! I hope Amelia pays dearly for this someday!" angrily muttered Chiarina.

On her way home from the piazza, Maddalena, for the first time since her wedding day, walked past the long, narrow stairway that had for so many years carried her away from Amelia to the joys and freedom of the piazza. This stairway had been the path for her and Cristoforo to escape to the Mound where they savored the stolen bread and consoled and comforted each other. Her heart ached for Cristoforo. She knew without her, he would suffer a dryness of spirit and a deep loneliness. She felt the same although her spirit felt cold and dead and her loneliness was so deep as to be unreachable.

She had arrived at the doorway of the store. As always her heart sank and she braced herself for what would come. She parted the beaded ropes hanging in the doorway and entered. The counter was empty and the house was quiet. She held her breath as footsteps sounded and Andrea appeared. His kindness warmed her for the moment. "Ah, *piccina*," he said, "give me the *conca*. You are needed in the kitchen."

Her many duties kept her busy, but one she truly dreaded— Saturday night. It was the custom in Sella di Corno that the men of the village gathered at the Chiuppi store to play cards, drink wine and eat sandwiches. As the wine began to take over, they would sometimes break out in creative versions of the village songs, or they could just as easily turn morose, angry and quarrelsome. One never knew which way it might go. Maddalena's job was to keep the wine flowing and the sandwiches at hand when the men called for them. Sometimes Massimo would humiliate her in front of his friends and she would rush out of the room in tears. The rest of the time her life revolved around helping in the house or occasionally working the counter in the store. Her only solace was the moments she stole to visit with Cristoforo. She missed her daily contact with him.

In a few months, Maddalena felt the stirrings of new life inside her. Anna Felice had been right—it all happened just the way she said it would. On March 5, 1910, her first child, Silia, was born. Maddalena was enchanted by her baby. Her loving nature, held back for so long by closed doors, now exploded into an open expression of her motherhood.

"Cristoforo," she whispered when she could take him aside for a moment, "my baby is the joy of my life." Cristoforo was happy for her. Noticing the smile under the sad eyes, he was grateful. He knew what a price she paid every day of her life.

Cristoforo also had changed. He was taller and stronger. He rarely smiled, and his dark eyes were steady, hard, and cold. He held his body in a rigid stance like a bow, ready to release an arrow. At fifteen, he was expected to carry a man's load of work, which developed not only his physical strength, but also a focused discipline that served him the rest of his life.

Cristoforo avoided Nonna Amelia as much as possible, but his hatred for her final cruelty in forcing Maddalena's marriage to Massimo burned in his eyes and in his cold, quiet rejection of her. Neither his father nor his grandfather could influence his low opinion of her. His heart ached from the pain she had inflicted on the sister he so loved. He would never forgive her.

Michele, on the other hand, was now stronger, although never up to his brother's ability. He was quicker to smile than his brother or sister. He was given lighter work—tending the mules, helping with household chores, and shopping at the Chiuppi store. Maddalena was always happy to see him and glad that Nonna Amelia treated him well. Her heart was full of love for him, and she did not resent his special treatment.

The village women welcomed Maddalena at the well and took her into their hearts. They fully understood her daily torment, and they rejoiced with her in her new motherhood. Concetta and Chiarina who had grieved about the marriage, now oo-ed and aah-ed over the baby, Silia. They all knew that Massimo's parents, Carolina and Andrea, were kindly people who tried to offset their son's unreasonable rages, and they were also delighted with the new grandchild.

Two years later Massimo announced that he, his wife and their little child, along with his younger brother, Giulio, would immigrate to America. Although his sister, Anna Felice, had settled in New York, Massimo planned to go to Chicago, where their friends Felicetta and

Assunta were living. At first, Maddalena was thrilled at the thought of seeing her friends again, but then she was horrified when she realized Cristoforo would be staying behind. At least here in Italy, she had Cristoforo to turn to, and they could talk. She felt powerless. She had all she could do to handle her husband, her child, her house, and working in the store. On top of all of that, she was pregnant again. She dared not dwell on the loss of Cristoforo, the one person who truly loved her. It was more than she could bear. She was only nineteen, and a future in a strange country terrified her. Cristoforo was devastated. What would his beloved sister do without his protection, little as it was?

Pulling himself together, he tried to comfort her. "You know, I'm seventeen now," he reminded her. "I have to leave for my two-year military service, and we would have been separated anyway." His words did not help. She feared for his safety, but at least they would have been in the same country.

As they prepared to leave, the townspeople recounted the tragic stories of people who did not survive the terrible conditions on the ship. Others recalled stories of the people who were turned back for various reasons and had to make the arduous trip back to Italy. In spite of it all, Massimo booked their passage on the German ship, Frederick the Great. They would leave on July 26, 1912, from the port of Naples.

Carolina and Andrea watched as Massimo and Giulio prepared to leave the village. Their sons had been so difficult, they almost felt a sense of relief to see them go. However, since Bettina had moved to Tornimparte and Anna Felice had already gone to America, the store would become more of a burden. They would just have to manage one way or another.

The Ferrara family said their goodbyes privately—Nonna Amelia was curt, but Nonna Cristoforo and Babbo Francesco hugged Maddalena tightly. Michele wept. Cristoforo was dry-eyed, his heart broken. Maddalena stoically received each person's contribution. For her, the worst had already happened. Everything else would just be more of the same to be endured.

On the day before the departure, the villagers turned out to say their goodbyes and to give their well wishes. The women looked at Maddalena, her slight figure rounding with new life, and her sweet face dominated by eyes that were dark pools of sadness, and they cried inside for her. The handsome Massimo, arrogantly pronouncing the great life they had ahead of them, left them cold, considering the havoc he left behind and the possibility of even more in Maddalena's future. Only the little Silia, at two years of age, delighted everyone with her joy of living.

When everyone had finished their goodbyes, Maddalena and Cristoforo found a way to meet at the Mound. They sat, silenced by their pain. The valley below glowed in the late afternoon sun, each patchwork field gently waving in the breeze. Over the fields, the mountains stood firm, strong, and protective. Maddalena was the first to speak. "Don't worry, Cristoforo. I'll be all right," she said, her voice gently penetrating his fierce anger and hopeless sadness.

Like the mountains, he wanted to surround her with his strength and protect her from the life that awaited her. He would find a way, somehow. In a cracked voice, he replied, "When I come back from my military duty in two years, I will go to America and find you." In as comforting a voice as he could muster, he added, "We will be together again." They sat silently for a while. Then, without another word or physical gesture, they rose and together walked home.

Very early the next morning, the carriage pulled up in front of the Chiuppi store. The trip to Rome would take a full day. As the baggage was loaded, the children danced around the horses and tried to get up on the driver's seat. As Maddalena climbed into the carriage, she stopped a moment to find Cristoforo, but he was nowhere in sight. She understood, and quietly settled herself with baby Silia on her lap. Once Massimo was in, the word was given to the driver, and the carriage took off.

Chapter Eleven

After arriving in Rome, they spent the night at an inn to rest, and the next morning set off for Naples to board the ship. The previous day had been exhausting, and little Silia was cranky and overtired, so the early departure was difficult. It was Maddalena's first trip away from the village, and she found the city of Rome overwhelming. So many people, so many buildings.

As the carriage left the city for Naples, a new countryside opened up. Instead of the familiar mountains of the Apennines, flat open fields stretched out with farmhouses strewn here and there, with strange shapes of haystacks dotting the fields. The road was rough, the carriage extremely uncomfortable, and both brothers and Silia were constantly complaining. Maddalena did her best to keep things calm by giving the child tidbits of food and ignoring the tirades of the others.

They finally entered Naples, and the raucousness of the city came as another shock. Again they took a room at an inn close to the port, but it was literally impossible to sleep because the people in the town never seemed to go home. The next morning Maddalena was stunned to see the immense ship they were going to board. Her senses could not take in the breadth and height of it. There was pandemonium in the port—people yelling at each other and vendors selling objects in a singsong dialect she did not understand. Hordes of people were pushing and pulling in all directions. It seemed complete chaos after the peaceful serenity of Sella di Corno.

They finally left the busy port and struggled up the gangplank to board the ship. The passengers were packed shoulder to shoulder and elbowed each other so it was hard for Maddalena to move freely and keep track of the two-year-old Silia. Massimo and Giulio carried their bags and did their share of the pushing and pulling.

When they were finally on-board and directed to their quarters, Maddalena gasped with horror. They were at the very bottom of the ship and everyone was shoved against each other. There was barely room to move. The unceasing drone of the engines created a dull roar that constantly assailed their ears. The dim light made it hard to see. The air was still and stale. People were panicked and began to mutter complaints. "Is this what our ticket bought us?" While they maneuvered to find an advantageous spot, some angrily cursed the Italian government that made it necessary for them to leave, the ship company that took their money and threw them into this hell hole, and the overall bad luck that pursued them everywhere.

The misery of stale, smelly air was relieved by an occasional allowance to go out on a lower deck for a brief respite. Like animals that had been kept in a sealed enclosure, they gulped in the fresh ocean air, moved freely about and stretched their legs. They gazed at the sun, their eyes roving over its light shining on the water—all in a desperate attempt to soak up as much as possible before returning to the bowels of the ship.

Nothing, however, could improve the flavorless soup served out of huge metal containers. Poor as they might have been in Italy, they had always managed to make flavorful food, often eating from their own gardens and butchering their own chickens and rabbits.

Maddalena tried to comfort herself with visions of the sea and sand of Vasto and the pure mountain air and blue sky of Sella de Corno. However, the reality of Silia tugging at her and constantly demanding her attention kept her memories at bay. Her pregnancy made it difficult for her to sit comfortably anywhere. Massimo found some cronies and spent his time playing cards, completely detached from the needs of his wife and child. Although some of the women tried to help her, she keenly felt the loss of her friends and most of all her brother, Cristoforo. There was no way to run to the Mound for comfort. Her isolation engulfed her. Would this ever end?

The two weeks at sea felt like two centuries. When word finally came that they were approaching America, the misery of it all dropped away as everyone cheered. Their rescue was at hand—the <u>Promised Land</u>! Everything was going to be all right. Yet the joy was tinged with fear. They had heard that people were turned back at Ellis Island for minor diseases and forced to make the voyage back to Italy. That would be pure hell, and no one could completely be free until they had passed through the immigration process. They now understood why Ellis Island was called *Isola delle Lagrime* (the island of tears).

As each ferry left the ship for the island, everyone cheered and called out, "*Buona fortuna.*" Then they restlessly waited for their turn. Finally, Maddalena and Massimo were called. Giulio helped them gather up their belongings, and with Silia in tow, they boarded the ferry.

The ride to Ellis Island was bumpy, but no one complained. A quiet fell over the group. Now the reality of facing the immigration process weighed on them, and they grew silent. Fear was palpable. No one knew what to expect.

Once on the island, they had no time to think. They had to move from line to line—to answer questions regarding the past and the future, to be re-questioned if necessary and double-checked for health problems. Once the movement through the lines was completed, the last question was the intended destination. Massimo answered, "Chicago," and they were then led to the ferry that would take them to Hoboken, New Jersey, where they would board a train to Chicago.

Family Locations

Vasto, Italy

"The Mound" Sella di Corno, Italy

Women in Piazza

Charcoal Making Process

Chiuppi Store/Home

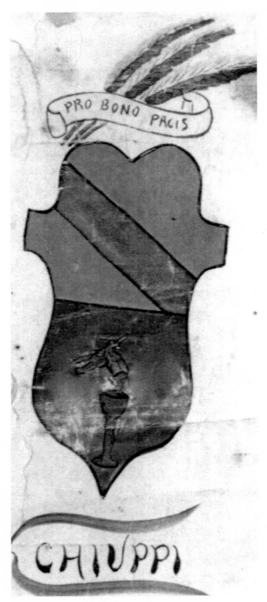

Chiuppi Family Crest

Silia & Maddalena

Massimo

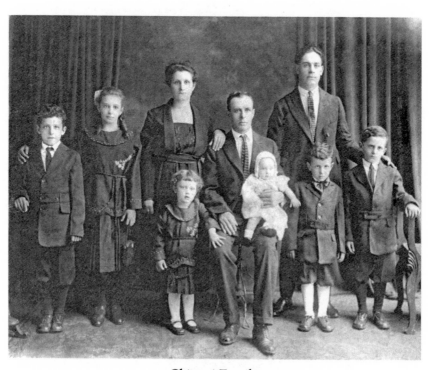

Chiuppi Family:
Andrew, Silia, Maddalena, Massimo, Giulio,
(front) Angelina, Clara, Frank, Enrico
(all in rented clothes)

Anna Felice & Angelina

Angelina & Assunta's daughter, Pietrina

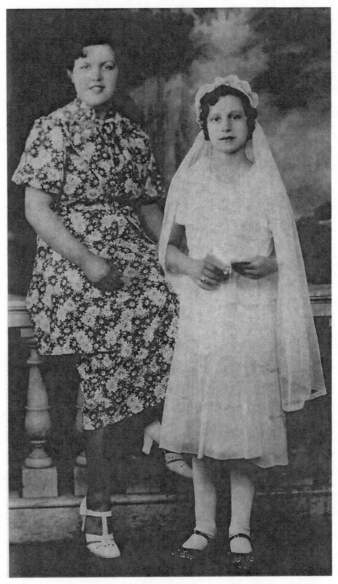

Ida, Felicetta's daughter, and Caroline

Michael & Maddalena

Enrico, Andrew & Michael

Frank & Jim

Clara, Silia, Maddalena, Caroline, Angelina

Maddalena & Cristoforo

Cristoforo "Stone House" Arkansas

Maddalena & Grandchild

Maddalena & Staff at Saint Francis

Part II

Chicago

1912

"They tell me you are wicked and I believe them, for I have seen your painted women under the gas lamps luring the farm boys.

And they tell me you are crooked and I answer: Yes, it is true I have seen the gunman kill and go free to kill again.

And they tell me you are brutal and my reply is: On the faces of women and children I have seen the marks of wanton hunger.

And having answered so I turn once more to those who sneer at this my city, and I give them back the sneer and say to them:

Come and show me another city with lifted head singing so proud to be alive and coarse and strong and cunning."

—from *Chicago*, by Carl Sandburg

Chapter Twelve

With a profound fatigue overcoming her, Maddalena settled herself into a seat on the train. At last—a place to sit, fresh air to breathe, and daylight shining all around her to enjoy. The nightmare of the past two weeks began to fade. All the events that had taken place since they left Sella di Corno tumbled around in her mind. Until the age of nineteen, she had left her village only to go to Vasto, had never been on a train or a ship, and had never seen a city or huge crowds of people. Her life had centered around the few families in the village, the church, the piazza with her friends, the Mound with Cristoforo, and home with Nonno and Babbo. She tried not to think of Amelia, her step-grandmother, or her concerns about Cristoforo, who would be leaving for his two-year military duty.

So many things were new to her that she felt a chaotic jumble that had begun with her first view of Rome, then of the port of Naples, the horrors of the ship, the lines in Ellis Island, and now a train carrying her to a strange city. She shook off her thoughts and turned to discover that Silia had taken off to run up and down the aisles of the train. Massimo was dozing in his seat. As she went down the aisle to retrieve the child, the movement of the train almost knocked her over. The conductor helped steady her, and her heart surged with thanks. "The Americans are nice," she thought. Little Silia was having fun—people were talking to her and smiling at her. Again, Maddalena felt, "These are good people; everything will be all right." Back in her seat, she managed to get

Silia to nap, and with a new hope in her heart, she herself succumbed to her exhaustion and fell into a deep sleep.

Back in Italy, Cristoforo mourned for his sister. After the carriage had left Sella di Corno, he went to the Mound and sat alone. Maddalena's absent presence was almost palpable. His grief surrounded him like a heavy curtain shutting off any penetration of warmth or light. In his frozen stillness, the buried ache of the loss of his mother re-emerged and joined the present ache of the loss of his beloved sister, the sister in whom he had found the only warmth and love that kept his spirit alive. Now he was really alone.

The bleating of some sheep in the distance, the gentle rustling of the leaves in the trees barely touched his consciousness. The cool breeze brushed his body, but he felt and heard nothing. He had lost everything, and life would never be the same. He would cut off his feelings and after his military duty was finished, he would go to America to find Maddalena. He knew the hell she would have to live through under Massimo's unrelenting attacks, and he would do everything he could to relieve and comfort her.

With this goal in mind, he pulled himself up and stood for a while looking over the verdant valleys below. His spare frame took on a tight, resolute, contained stance that would present him throughout his life as a "no nonsense" person.

As he walked down from the Mound and reached the village, he welcomed the thought of leaving in a few days for the north of Italy to the Veneto region where he would spend his two years of military service. There was nothing to hold him here.

Maddalena awoke to the voice of the conductor announcing the next stop—Chicago. The excitement again mounted and the next thing she knew they were standing on the platform outside the train station. Massimo and Giulio stood surrounded by their baggage. Massimo stared at the piece of paper he had carefully saved. People hurried by, jostling him in their rush to get to the station. He swore at them in Italian. Maddalena waited for his next move as she comforted the tired, restless child.

They were to be met at the station by her dear childhood friends, Felicetta, and her husband, Paolo Mangini, who would guide them to the flat they had rented for them next to their own at 915 Hermitage Avenue. As soon as the crowd thinned, Massimo and Giulio gathered up their bags and, with Maddalena pulling Silia with one hand and holding bags in the other, they made their way along the platform to the station. Maddalena felt desperately tired and stretched to her limit as she sought to keep up with the impatient Massimo. The new life stirring within her cried for food and rest. She felt the full impact of the series of events that had led from Sella di Corno to this moment in the train station. The train ride had been a short respite, but now she felt that she could not take another step.

Seemingly out of nowhere, she heard a shout. "Paolo," yelled Massimo. Through the crowd she caught a glimpse of Paolo and Felicetta. She was unable to move, and fell on one of the suitcases into a fit of uncontrollable tears. She sat and wept until Massimo angrily yanked her up and yelled, *"Ma stupida, fa la finita!"*

Paolo came up to them with Felicetta in tow. Felicetta grabbed the shaken Maddalena and held her tight while they both wept.

"Maddalena, I am so happy to see you safe and sound," Felicetta whispered. But Maddalena could not find the strength or the words to respond. Soon, Massimo's voice broke in, harshly demanding to get on with it. They broke apart, divided the baggage and packages, and with Silia tucked into Felicetta's arms, began their way out of the station.

For the first time, Maddalena became aware of her surroundings. The cavernous lobby of the station, the raucous reverberation of sounds of people calling out to each other or yelling at ticket agents to make themselves heard, the push and pull of people trying to make their way, all fell on her like a huge weight. She hugged the packages she was carrying tightly as if to balance all the outer influences that were pulling her apart.

They finally reached the doorway and emerged from the station into the Chicago streets. Suddenly a great gust of wind threw Maddalena completely off balance. Her packages went flying in all directions as she fell to the ground. She tried to lift herself up and brace herself against the wind. At the same time she recoiled against the verbal tirade Massimo sent in her direction. He and Paolo set their bags down to recover hers, but they too had to fight the power of the Chicago wind. It was a force they had never experienced. Massimo, resigning himself to her inability to manage, relieved her of carrying anything and ordered her to hang on to Felicetta, who with Silia on one arm, anchored Maddalena with the other. Thus rearranged, they began the two-mile walk to their new home in Chicago's Near West Side.

Through the mist of her exhaustion and the efforts to overcome the wind, the sights, sounds, and smells of the city unmercifully pierced through to her core, and she became aware that the street was jammed with crowds of people, hurrying and scurrying in every direction with unseeing eyes but relentless purpose. Some rushed to board the open electric streetcars, which themselves made screeching sounds at every start and stop. Every time a rider scrambled aboard the rear platform and paid his seven cents, the conductor noisily rang it up on a large register. This continued until the last person paid; then he yanked a bell cord twice, giving the motorman at the other end of the car the signal to start up again. She could hardly keep her eyes off these scarlet and cream elongated cars that magically moved on tracks, loaded with people. The streets were also filled with horses and wagons carrying loads, the horses' hooves clip-clopping against the road. Trucks rumbled by. Occasionally horns from automobiles added to the unceasing din.

Maddalena looked for Massimo and Paolo. They were barely visible ahead, separated by the flow of people. It was hard for the little group to stay together. A sudden jostling of the crowd almost pushed her away from Felicetta. Filled with fear, she clung more tightly to her friend's arm, realizing that if she lost that anchor, she would be swept away into the crowd as a pebble would be carried along in a fast river. She would be lost in a strange country.

Her senses deluged by the sounds from the teeming streets, the crowds on the sidewalks, the smell of horse dung and the fear of being lost, Maddalena longed to escape to the peaceful Mound to sit with

Cristoforo overlooking the serene valleys and gazing at the silent mountains and open sky.

They threaded their way through the crowds moving along the streets that made up Chicago's Loop: Dearborn, Clark, State, La Salle, and the dark alleyways of the financial business district of downtown Chicago. From each side of the streets rose towering dark buildings, one next to the other, for blocks on end, obscuring the sun and sometimes causing wind tunnels which slowed the crowd as it struggled to move forward. No blade of grass could stake its claim here. No tree could bend to the wind. Here was a man-made forest; pillars of concrete rising to the sky, darkening their base where the people who walked could see only a ribbon strip of blue sky if they tipped their heads backwards. The little group struggled to stay within visual distance of each other, but was constantly thwarted by impatient people irritated by any slower moving force. Silia began to fret. Felicetta began to feel the weight of the responsibility each arm bore. Maddalena dragged her weary body with a terrified hold on the trusted arm of her friend. It felt unending as they plugged along, block after block until finally, the crowds began to thin out, the buildings lost some of their height, and they found themselves at the outskirts of the downtown area. They were able to stay closer together now and even stopped for a moment to set Silia on the ground for a little run around. The remaining journey moved through a variety of neighborhoods where they saw stands selling fruit and vegetables, Mom and Pop stores selling groceries, bakeries, and butcher shops. Interspersed with these were run-down bungalows and brick apartment buildings.

"It's not too much farther," encouraged Paolo in a gentle voice as he observed the exhausted Maddalena. The antithesis of Massimo, Paolo was a soft-spoken man with a kind face and an open heart. He and Felicetta were well matched. Both understood and supported Maddalena in the dilemma that faced her, but were careful not to antagonize Massimo with that support.

Maddalena loosened her grip on Felicetta's arm. Her fear lifted, and she felt free to breathe again and to look around. She was struck by the flatness of the city. The straight lines of the streets went on endlessly in every direction. There were no shapes against the sky to tease the eye upward. No valleys below to entice one to cast a lowered glance. The blare and roar of the downtown area became a lively, active assortment of sounds; peddlers called out their wares; drivers directed their horses as they carried their loads down the street. There were no street cars with their intrusive noise. Loose groups of people came and went, shopping and visiting. Suddenly, her ear caught the sound of Italian being spoken as passersby conversed with each other. She looked up at Felicetta. "Did you hear that?" she asked.

Felicetta smiled and said, "Your new home is right around the corner."

The wind had died down. They turned the corner easily and found themselves on Hermitage Avenue. The street was dominated by several two or three-storied brick buildings with residential flats, various types of wood structures that served as single family cottages, and an occasional empty lot where children were playing games.

It was a beautiful September afternoon as only Chicago's Indian summers could provide. The street seemed to come alive. Small groups of people were gathered here and there in casual conversation. Others sat on their front stoops or stairs and visited with each other, interrupting their talks to greet passersby. Everywhere children with screaming voices called out in their play.

The weary group was given curious glances as they walked. Maddalena noticed a large group in front of a brick building and as they drew closer, that group broke up and rushed toward them. *"Benvenuto, benvenuto"* (welcome, welcome), they called out in happy shouts. They were soon engulfed with hugs, relieved of packages and baggage and practically pushed forward into the brick building.

Inside the second-story flat, they were greeted by a smaller group. Here, Assunta, Felicetta's sister, had laid out a table of food and as they entered, they were told to sit and rest and eat. "At last!" Maddalena thought as she wearily sank into the nearest chair. Immediately, someone brought her a drink and a plate of food. She was so weak she could barely bring the fork to her mouth or the glass to her lips. She wanted only to go to bed and sleep for a long time.

Mixed in with the eating and greeting, a multitude of questions were thrown at them. "How was it on the ship? How are the folks in the village at home? Who got married? Who died? Were any babies born?" They were hungry for news of the old country. All of these were answered by Massimo, who gloried in all the attention and held forth with much gusto.

Maddalena sat in a stupor, feeling the life inside her and trying to eat something to support that life. She barely noticed the people around her, only that Felicetta, her dear friend, hovered over her, pushing her to eat.

As people finished their food and got their questions answered, they began slowly to say their goodbyes, which were delayed, since every new thought or question had to be expressed at length. When the last *addio* was said, Assunta began to clear the table. Paola and Massimo picked up the bags and followed as Felicetta led Maddalena to their flat.

The building had six flats set up in three stories with three flats in the front and three in the rear. Paolo had rented the second-story rear for the newcomers. The flats were entered by a side walkway from the street leading to the center of the building. A stairway then offered entrances to each flat from a central hallway. The rear flats opened up at the back to a large porch facing the alley. Stairways led from each porch down to the walkway to the street.

After everyone else had left, Maddalena, Massimo, and little Silia, along with Felicetta, crossed the central hallway from the front to the rear flat. It was sparsely furnished with only the basic necessities. They entered a small hall leading into the living room which held two chairs, then into a dining room which was empty, and finally into a kitchen. The kitchen had a table and chairs, a coal stove for heating and cooking, and an icebox. Off each room was a bedroom and between the last two bedrooms, a small bathroom. The bedroom off the kitchen had a bed and a dresser.

Maddalena was too numb with fatigue to see anything. With infinite weariness she allowed Felicetta to lead her to the bedroom, where she fell on the bed with a thud. All too soon she felt the sudden weight of his heavy body on top of her. She lay there helplessly.

Chapter Thirteen

Cristoforo stepped out of the train station and gasped at the beauty of his new home. The assignment for his two-year military duty had brought him to the Veneto region of northern Italy. He was to be trained and then serve with the famous Alpini regiment. As he glanced around, his thoughts flew back for the moment to Sella di Corno and the rugged Apennine mountains that he and Maddalena had enjoyed together. Beautiful as those mountains were, they could not compare to what he saw before him now. The majesty of the Dolomites and the distant Alps held him rooted and silent.

When he left Sella di Corno, he was depressed. The painful separation from his sister had devastated him. He would miss her love and support. Worse than this loss, however, was having to watch helplessly as she left for America in the hands of Massimo. His determination to find her and stand beside her in her struggle grew stronger. Yet he knew that until he was freed from his two-year duty, he could do nothing. Little did he know that World War I would take up another four years of his life, that he would don the cap of the Alpini cavalry soldiers with the famous black feather attached, and fight the Turks. Later, he would also fight to wrench the Trentino-Alto Adige and the northern Veneto regions from the Austrians. However, with none of this future known to him, his thoughts centered on finding the training station and reporting for duty.

He easily fit in with the disciplined routine and the rigid structure of the military. His "no nonsense" persona, his stern, serious and unsmiling face did not encourage an easy exchange with his fellow trainees. When off duty, he rarely went on the sprees that the others looked forward to. Not having attended school in Sella di Corno, he put his attention on learning to read. His short furloughs were spent exploring the towns and the countryside, which offered a landscape so different from his in the Abruzzo region.

Picturesque villages were scattered throughout the area, nestled in valleys or perched on the sides of mountains. He was enchanted by the castles and by the churches with onion-shaped domes. He hiked the mountains and strolled through the villages, stopping for his afternoon coffee in a people-watching outdoor café. These were the moments when he felt some relief from his nagging unhappiness.

He discovered that singing made him happy. The Alpine regiment had a song that was their very own, which they sang frequently:

"On our cap there is a black feather
That serves as a banner,
For the Alpine soldiers.
Long live the regiment
Long live the Alpine corps soldiers!"

When he sang along with the men, he felt less isolated; his spirit quickened and an inner smile formed in his soul. They teased him, "Ah, Cristoforo, you are a hidden artist." He only shook his head and did not encourage the conversation. They sang many songs, and he learned them all. For the rest of his life he would turn to singing to soothe the deep sorrow within him. In singing he would find solace, comfort and a loosening of the tightness of his inner core.

His superiors were very pleased with his work. He set himself to each task with fierce concentration and vigor and went far beyond the requirements. This set him apart even further from the others. Life fell into a pattern of study and training for the next two years.

News from Sella di Corno trickled in from time to time. He learned that Michele was much stronger and had taken over Cristoforo's duties with the caravan. However, Michele was approaching seventeen, and he too would soon be leaving for his military duty.

This was not good news for Michele. He had fallen in love with the town beauty, Elena, and they were engaged. Michele became inconsolable when he received the notice that he also would be sent to the north for his training. Only the possibility of seeing his brother made it somewhat easier to leave his fiancée.

As Cristoforo began to make up his plans to return to Sella di Corno in the final days of his duty, war clouds began to gather in Europe. All soldiers were frozen in their positions pending the outcome. It was not long before a full-blown war was declared—World War I. Italy would begin to fight the Austrians in the region where Cristoforo was and where Michele would soon arrive. Cristoforo was nineteen, Michele was seventeen. During the next four years, Cristoforo would fight for his country and then return to Sella di Corno. Michele, however, would fight and die for his country and be buried in northern Italy in the Trentino area.

Chapter Fourteen

Several months after their arrival, Maddalena gave birth to the baby she carried on the long journey from Sella di Corno to Chicago. They named him Andrew, after Massimo's father. The child was not strong, had many colds and demanded a lot of attention. To her consternation, when he was only six months old, she was pregnant again.

She asked herself, "How can I care for another child when I can hardly meet the needs of the ones I already have?" The daily struggle was draining her. The dribbles of money that came in from the occasional bricklaying jobs Paolo found for Massimo barely put a dent in their needs, especially since Massimo carefully subtracted part of what he earned for his cigars, his wine, and Fernet-Branca, (an Italian herbal digestive) he had to have with his breakfast. There was never enough to cover the rent, food, and heat. In order to survive, they finally had to apply to the government for relief. At least, she could then count on a monthly supply of beans, cheese, and flour. With help from Felicetta and Assunta, she managed to get through the pregnancy as she cared for the sickly Andrew and the toddler Silia.

Massimo insisted the new baby be named after his uncle, Enrico. Although Maddalena knew that Massimo's mother Carolina Manzara had two brothers, Enrico and Angelino, they both had moved to other villages and were rarely part of family activities in Italy. It was known that they were married, had small children, and were considering immigrating to America. It mattered little to Maddalena what the child was named. She would love the child regardless.

One day, Paolo and Felicetta rushed into the apartment full of excitement.

"I have the perfect job for Massimo," said Paolo, with Felicetta beaming at his side. Maddalena carrying Enrico in her arms led them to the kitchen where they sat down to hear the good news.

"What is it? What is it?" she clamored.

"Well," Paolo began, "one of the men in the neighborhood heard that a local business was hiring. It's the J. B. Simpson Company. They're looking for tailors."

"What better job for Massimo," happily added Felicetta, "with his training and experience in Italy."

"And," added Paolo, "this would be a steady job, five days a week." Maddalena stared at them—a job—five days a week—money coming in regularly. It was too much good news to absorb. She felt elated.

"Paolo, Felicetta, how can I thank you. Just think, more food, warm clothes, and enough coal to keep the apartment warm. It will help us all but especially poor little Andrew. I am so happy," and she gave them a warm smile. Everyone felt the joy of the moment.

As Paolo left, he said, "I'll be back tonight to talk to Massimo." The two women shared the remaining part of the afternoon.

As Felicetta prepared to leave, she said to her friend, "Things are going to be better." Maddalena glowed with anticipation. That evening Paolo returned to give Massimo the good news. Massimo shrugged, and agreed to try it.

The J. B. Simpson Company made men's suits and topcoats. The company worked on the piecework system where each man sewed a separate item: one man, a collar; another, a sleeve; another, a lapel. The pieces were brought to a central location where they were assembled to complete the final garment. Each man received a ticket for the items he completed. At the end of the week, all of his tickets were placed in his individual notebook, which was presented to the floor man as proof of the work he had accomplished. He was then paid according to the number of tickets he produced. The whirr of 50 sewing machines; the dust that accumulated from minute scraps of fabric; the constant repetitive motion needed to produce the item; all of this irritated Massimo. "Is this what I learned to do in Italy—sit like a statue and do the same thing over and over?" he grumbled. He lasted two days. Giving no thought to the needs of his family, he walked off the job.

Maddalena was horrified. What would they do now? Paolo assured her there would be something else. He would look.

Chapter Fifteen

Three years later, Maddalena was pregnant again. She did not welcome it. Silia was now seven, Andrew was four, and Enrico was almost three. Silia was a quiet child, but Andrew and Enrico, born only thirteen months apart, demanded every moment of her attention. Recently she had awakened in terror to hear Andrew gasping for breath. They had no telephone. Massimo rushed to Felicetta's flat for help. By the time she arrived, Maddalena had the child swaddled in blankets at the front door. Instinctively she knew he had to be in a hospital. Paolo joined them as they all ran the six blocks to get to the Cook County Hospital. Felicetta remained behind, taking the other children to her flat. The doctors told them that Andrew had diphtheria and also suffered from undernourishment. They warned that after treatment, he would most likely have a chronic lung condition and need high quality nutrition to support his health. Maddalena loved her children and reveled in their growth, but she was also continually exhausted and stressed. No consistent money came into the house to support them. How would she be able to give her son what he needed?

Several weeks later, the neighborhood was abuzz with excitement—Massimo's uncles, Angelino and Enrico, would be arriving from Italy. The talk ran through the everyday life of the neighborhood. Would they make it on the ship for the two weeks in steerage? Would they make it through Ellis Island? Although the newcomers already had a place to live on Grand Avenue, it was a concern because it was outside the Italian neighborhood where security and comfort came from following the old country traditions. Grand Avenue, however, was in a business district. Day to day, the neighbors asked each other the same questions and relived their own past experiences, going through the entire process over and over. When the word came that the uncles had arrived and made it through, everyone celebrated. When their train arrived at the Dearborn Street railroad station many were there to welcome them. Others gathered at their new home to prepare food and listen to their story.

Massimo was not pleased with his uncles' arrival. They had often berated him for his treatment of his mother. He had lifted his hand to her, and his rages had caused his parents much grief. Massimo felt no connection to these uncles and wished they had stayed in the old country. Since Massimo left the J.B. Simpson Company, Paolo was able to find only day jobs for him as a bricklayer. It was hard physical labor, which he was not used to, and again, repetitive work bored and irritated him. He was used to the freedom of movement in the grocery store back in Italy and control over his relationships with the customers. His arrogance and snide remarks had never been confronted in Sella di Corno, but here his employers told him not to return.

Maddalena was ready to deliver, and they had no money to pay the midwife. Felicetta and Paolo talked it over. "We must help her," they agreed. But Paolo added, "I can't keep finding him jobs forever. Why won't he stay on the job whether he likes it or not? He has a family to feed." Paolo was perplexed.

"It's a boy!" the midwife said. They called the fourth child Frank, after Maddalena's father, Francesco. Felicetta and Assunta helped as much as they could. Neighbors brought over food. People began to realize the severe strains that Massimo's inability to keep a job were placing on the growing family. Massimo himself saw nothing. He spent his time away from home in random activities. On weekends, he met with his cronies to play cards and drink.

When they could no longer pay the rent, Angelino stepped in. He and Enrico found a grocery store for rent with living quarters above it. It was close to where they lived. The two uncles talked it over. Maybe

Massimo would be more successful back in a business he was used to. They agreed to help him out for six months until they could get the store going.

Felicetta and Paolo were sad as they watched their friends prepare to leave Hermitage Avenue. Felicetta particularly suffered the loss of her friend but more, the loss of the support and daily assistance she could give her when they lived close by. Paolo worried that his unspoken influence over Massimo to curb some of his behavior would be gone. He knew that the uncles had no control over Massimo. They feared for Maddalena.

Chapter Sixteen

Little did they know when they had walked from the Dearborn station upon their arrival from Italy that they were walking to the Near West Side—the worst neighborhood in Chicago for poverty and crime. The area was on the edge of downtown, bordered by 12th Street to the south, later called Roosevelt Road, and West Madison to the north, the Skid Row of Chicago. Running west from downtown for approximately three miles was Taylor Street, the center of Italian-American neighborhood life. An offshoot of this area was West Grand Avenue, slightly north of West Madison Street.

Massimo pulled the horse and wagon in front of the building where his two uncles lived. After tying the horses up, he helped Maddalena and the four children off the wagon, leaving beds, small pieces of furniture, and suitcases to be unloaded later with his uncles' help. This would be the first of many trips to transfer their belongings and set up the new living quarters. Filomena, Enrico's wife, welcomed them in and served them a bountiful lunch of minestrone, pasta, and Italian sausage. She loved to prepare food for everyone, so her home became a refuge for the children who also got to know Tony, their only child. The cousins played together and Filomena was happy to have them at her house.

"You must come often," said Filomena, as she dished out the food. A grateful Maddalena smiled, as she watched the children hungrily fill up on the good food.

"Yes," continued Filomena. "Tony gets lonely." At this point,

Angelino's wife came in with their two children, Fred and Jack. She was nicknamed '*La Romana*' (the Roman) for her air of superiority, having been born in Rome, whereas the other Italians were from the deep south. The children were the same ages as Andrew and Enrico, so later, she would often pick them up and take them to her flat to play with their cousins, giving Maddalena much needed respite.

As they settled into 1465 West Grand Avenue, Maddalena was in shock. Having left a quiet, community-oriented street on Hermitage, she had not expected the noisy, chaotic, busy street they now lived on. Streetcars constantly ran up and down, making a clanging and noisy din. Pool halls and businesses dominated the street, creating a parade of strangers who came and went. The pool halls served liquor, and often, drunks would weave up and down the street. Neon signs blinked on and off, advertising the brands of beer served. The pool halls were the bottom level of the criminal organizations and often the hangouts for the gangs' gunmen. Mixed in between the pool halls and businesses were a variety of two and three-storied buildings with residential flats. Angelino and Enrico lived on the second floor of one of these buildings. A long dark stairway led up to their almost windowless flat—windowless due to the row house construction of the buildings.

Down the street from their flat was the grocery store they rented for Massimo and Maddalena. On the large display window, block letters spelled out ITALIAN GROCERIES. Inside the window a variety of pastas were arranged surrounded by wheels of black-coated hard cheese. The entrance led directly to a counter. Off the counter, to the right, was a glass-encased space with an assortment of Italian meats, prosciutto, mortadella and small hard salamis plus fresh mozzarella cheese in water and opened wheels of hard cheeses, provolone, parmigiano, and asiago. To the left of the counter was a scale. On the sides were bins filled with fresh fruits and vegetables, various barrels filled with assorted dried beans, dried salted cod (*bacala*), cured olives and shelves with cans of Mazola corn oil, olive oil, tomatoes, and tomato paste. Hanging from the ceiling were garlands of garlic, small roped hard cheeses, and sausages. As customers entered the store, the delicious aromas hit their nostrils, creating a mouth-watering need for samples.

To the rear of the store were storage areas and the entrance to the stairway leading to the living quarters. The upstairs flat was dark, with windows only at each end—one facing the street and the other facing the alley. The rooms were small and gave the children little space to play. Maddalena had to run the store when Massimo was away, and at those times, the children ran up and down the stairs except for Frankie, who was barely one year old. She would carry him to the storage room and set him down for a nap on a makeshift cot. Now Maddalena was faced with caring for the four children, cooking and cleaning, and working in the store. She had no time to worry about how she was going to do it or what should come first. She went from moment to moment frantically.

Massimo's trip to the market became a highlight for Andrew and Enrico as they grew older. At four in the morning, Massimo brought the horse and wagon in front of the store, and the boys climbed in next to their father. They loved the darkness of the night, the clatter and clop clop of the horses' hooves in the quiet street. An occasional streetcar went by, and a few people straggled along the sidewalk. Once they got to the market, Massimo haggled for the prices of the food, and the two boys watched as the back of the wagon was filled up with crates and boxes of fruits and vegetables. As they returned to the store, the morning light also returned, and the streets filled with people, more street cars, and other horses and wagons. The children helped unload whatever they could and rushed in to tell Maddalena all about the market. Silia hung in the background, quietly observing. Her share of the labor was unloading the cans and stacking them on the shelves. Once everything was unloaded and the horse and wagon returned to the stable, Massimo went back to bed and Maddalena opened up the store for business.

The customers loved Maddalena. Her sweet smile greeted them and her desire to be helpful was heart-warming. She was twenty-five years old, but her face showed a tension beyond those years. Customers noticed an inexplicable sadness in her eyes, and they wondered. When they saw that she was pregnant again, they shook their heads.

Massimo managed to find a space for a card table in the storage area and set it up for his weekend card games and drinking bouts with his friends. Maddalena ran the store when this took place. The addition of her pregnancy was wearing her down, and the new baby was born prematurely. They named him Angelo. He lived only forty days.

Felicetta and her sister, Assunta, had come to help after the delivery, but could only stay for one day. The seven-cent street car fare made too much of a dent in their budget to come more often, and it was too far to walk back and forth in one day. After baby Angelo died, they came again. Maddalena was inconsolable. She refused to eat and would barely talk. She could not cry. The two sisters begged her to let them take Frankie and Enrico back with them for a while to give her some rest, but she refused. They persisted and she finally gave in. As she watched her two sons leave, she feared she might lose them, too. A depression settled around her, and the customers missed her quiet smile. Massimo's only comment was *"Fa la finita"* (get over it).

Chapter Seventeen

When the letter came, Maddalena felt a jolt of anxiety. It was from Italy in Cristoforo's handwriting. Her anxiety and depression slowed her hand as she opened it. The mixed news broke the hold on her feelings. She sank to the floor and with her head on her lap, let go spasm after spasm of tears. The children rushed to her, but she ignored them. She cried out, "Michele, Michele" over and over. The words *"Michele fu ucciso in la guerra tre mese fa"* (Michele was killed in the war three months ago) tore into her. Her little brother. The gentle and delicate Michele she had guided up and down the narrow stairway to go to the piazza. The Michele who was able to stir some feeling in the heart of the cruel Amelia, their step-grandmother. The Michele that Babbo and Nonno so cherished; the Michele that she and Cristoforo had always protected—killed in the war. Killed in the war—the words beat on her brain with a rhythmic drumbeat.

Silia ran down to the store. "Papa, Papa—something is wrong with Mamma." But Massimo was unable to leave the counter unattended and besides he thought that she was acting crazy all the time anyhow. He ignored the children.

Even the good news that followed could not mitigate her suffering. Cristoforo was to marry Michele's fiancée, Elena, and they were planning to come to America as he promised. Massimo was not pleased. Having Cristoforo around would be a thorn in his side. Since their move from Hermitage Avenue, he was more and more irritated by the responsibilities laid on him by running the store. Without the curbing influence of Paolo, he unleashed his anger on Maddalena for every little thing. Too often, he would fly into a rage, storm up and down the stairs cursing her and her children, and finally walk out of the store. The children would huddle around their mother in fear while Maddalena steered them out of his way. After he left, she had no time to comfort them but brought them downstairs with her to tend to the customers. She tried to soothe them by giving them the Italian cookies they loved from the store's stock. She would like to have talked to Angelino or Enrico, but there was no phone. To send Silia on the busy street to get them was too dangerous. So, alone, she endured. There was no time to mourn her losses.

When Maddalena found out she was pregnant again, the pain of Angelo's death was somewhat relieved. She would bring Angelo back. She would re-name the new baby Angelo. When Massimo noticed her swelling belly, it meant nothing to him. However, Felicetta and Paolo were distressed. They saw changes in her. The sadness in her eyes deepened. Her shoulders were chronically crunched up toward her ears, as if to ward off a blow. She said very little to them when they came for an occasional visit. What was unchanged was the love she showered on her children. They were her joy. She was particularly happy to see Pietrina and Silia play together. Pietrina was Assunta's daughter and when the visits ended, Silia always cried. Occasionally Assunta would take Silia home with them, but Maddalena missed her too much and would say no to the next offer.

The bright spot in her life was the pending arrival of her brother. Cristoforo was only seventeen when they last saw each other—it was nine years ago. As her heart quickened, her brain raced with questions. What would he look like? He would be twenty-six. How much would he have changed, especially with his wartime experience? What would his wife be like?

A subsequent letter put a temporary end to the questions. It explained that they would not be coming because his wife, Elena, was pregnant and did not want to make the grueling trip until after the baby was born.

The store was becoming more and more of a problem. Her pregnancy, along with caring for the five children, kept her in such a state of exhaustion that she could not work at the counter as much as she had in the past. Massimo was furious. He raged at her constantly. He felt bound too tightly to the counter. His disinterest and erratic behavior cost them customers. He was unable to keep the accounts straight, and things began to fall into a chaotic jumble. When the baby was born, it was a girl. Maddalena's Angelo turned into Angelina. Massimo couldn't care less. He just wanted relief from attachment to the counter.

Felicetta and Paolo came one day and persuaded Maddalena to let them take Silia home with them for a few days. Pietrina had been asking for her friend to play with, and Maddalena was too tired to say "No." Zia 'La Romana' took Andrew and Enrico to play with their children at their flat, which left only Frankie and the baby for Maddalena to care for.

With the other children gone and Maddalena tending the baby, four-year-old Frankie wanted to spend all his time in the store with his father. But he irritated Massimo, who kept sending him back upstairs. Frankie would immediately go down the stairs again, and Massimo would drag him back up to his mother, screaming at Maddalena in Italian, "Keep your kid up there with you or there's going to be trouble."

Maddalena always cringed at his tone of voice. She would draw Frankie to her and begin to talk to him in a soothing voice. There were no toys to offer him, no way to send him out to play. She gave him cookies and tried to entertain him with stories she made up, using gestures and facial expressions. Things were getting so out of hand, and she did not know where to turn.

Chapter Eighteen

Six months later another letter came from Cristoforo. They would leave Italy with their baby girl, Liliana, in a week, arriving within a month if all went well. Liliana was the same age as Angelina. Maddalena could not contain her excitement. Her Cristoforo would soon be here. How she wished she could offer him her home, but they were crammed into very small rooms in a tiny dark flat. Since Zio Angelino and Zia Filamena had only one child, they had more space for the newcomers. She did not know how she would even find time to visit with Cristoforo. Massimo wanted her on the counter more and more. He had shouted several times, "*Basta!*"(enough). I have had it with this store. I am going to give it up and move to a flat."

The morning of the newcomers' arrival Maddalena was unable to greet them since she was working the counter while Massimo slept after going to market. Cristoforo, however, broke away to be with her. When he walked into the store and saw her behind the counter with the six-month-old Angelina on her arm and the four children scattered in the storage room, he stopped in his tracks in shock. He stepped to the side of the door to get out of the way of the customers and watched her make a sale. His heart ached for her. The frequent pregnancies, births, the death of Angelo and unrelenting abuses by Massimo showed in her physical appearance. Maddalena's face was pale, her shoulders more hunched, and her movements heavy and slow. She had gained weight, and it looked as though she could collapse at any time. But still she managed a weary smile for the customer as she completed the sale.

When she finally looked up and saw Cristoforo, she began to sob, deep sobs that shook her whole body. Steadying the baby on the counter she gave herself over to uncontrollable crying until he got to her side, and putting his arms around her, held her tightly. Neither of them could speak. Finally the baby's squirming brought them back into the moment. The children, hearing her cry, all gathered around and began to ask questions. Who was this man who made their mother cry? "This is your uncle Cristoforo," she told them, struggling to bring out the words. They soon lost interest and returned to their play.

Cristoforo and Maddalena faced each other. She looked at him and soaked in his presence. His usually serious face had taken on even more sternness and determination. His body was held in with an alert rigidity. But she saw none of this. She saw her beloved little brother who had fulfilled his promise to find her and protect her. She felt his love so deeply. She drank it in. It filled her parched soul. She put the "Closed" sign on the door, and they went back to the storage area. It was hard to find the words they wanted to say. Cristoforo spoke first. He took her hand.

"Maddalena, *finalmente*," (at last) he said.

The words would not come to her to respond. To quiet the squirming Angelina, she put her to her breast. At last, in a tight voice Maddalena uttered, "I have missed you." There were no smiles at this reunion. The sorrows they shared predominated. "And Michele?" she asked.

Cristoforo paused and then answered, "I never was able to see him. He is buried in Trentino."

They fell into silence. It was enough to be together. And then, the sounds of Massimo rising from sleep galvanized her into action.

"I must re-open the store," she said as she hurried to the front door and removed the "Closed" sign.

Cristoforo followed her to the door and, as he was leaving said, "I will come back later with Elena and the baby."

That evening Maddalena, Massimo and the children went to Zi'

Enrico and Zia Filomena's flat to visit. When they arrived, they found Zi' Angelino and Zia 'La Romana' there already. Maddalena looked at Cristoforo's wife in wonder. She was beautiful. She could see why Michele would fall in love with her and why Cristoforo would marry her. Their baby, Liliana, looked a lot like Cristoforo and when Maddalena picked her up, her ready smile touched Maddalena's heart. She and Cristoforo hardly spoke to each other, but they drank each other in with their eyes. Soon, the babble of all the children and the talk of the adults that grew louder and louder by the moment irritated Massimo, and he stood up to leave. Maddalena glanced sadly at Cristoforo and quietly followed her husband out the door.

Cristoforo was stunned by the contrast of life in Sella di Corno and the Veneto in Italy with life on the streets of west side Chicago. The beauties of nature that had fed him every day—the open sky, the fresh air, the rise and fall of the mountains and valleys, the colors of the day flowing into sunset, the nights with skies full of stars—these things were non-existent here. Instead, the ugliness of the city burned the souls of the people. Here, people were crammed together into tiny dark spaces, surrounded by buildings on top of buildings, surrounded by noise, streets full of people, strangers to each other. He had never seen anything like it. The war was bad, but this was another kind of war. The daily grind of poverty in the city with its unremitting struggle had none of the relief of the natural rewards of nature.

And to see Maddalena suffer—trapped, powerless under Massimo's constant attacks, inundated by responsibility—tore him apart. He so longed to take her away from it all. But there was no escape. If he could find a large flat and have her move in with his family, it would help. He knew Massimo was dissatisfied with the store and would not fight such a move. However, they would need more money than he was making as a day laborer, and he would have to ask Elena to go to work.

Elena balked at the idea. "But I have never worked," she answered, "besides, who would take care of the baby? I am afraid."

Cristoforo was firm in his decision. "You will learn what to do on the job, and Zia Filomena will tend to the baby. She has only one child and it will be easy for her," he informed her.

"But I don't want to," she pleaded. "Besides, who will nurse her? She is only six months old."

Cristoforo, still firm in his decision, responded, "Maddalena is nursing Angelina. She can also nurse Liliana." And with this, the discussion was ended.

Zia Filomena and Maddalena agreed to his terms, and a job was found for Elena. For the next year she worked in a factory close by. Zia 'La Romana' was incensed that the young mother was forced into leaving her child to go to work every day.

"Elena," she pounded at her daily, "you should not let him do this to you. Liliana needs her mother. Tell him you don't want to do it anymore."

The words fell on Elena's ears like the rain beating on a windowpane until finally her unhappiness broke through. She forced herself to face him. Speaking in as firm a voice as she could muster, she said, "Cristoforo, I cannot do this anymore. I want to go back to Italy."

Cristoforo, by this time, could see that the paltry income they made would never fulfill his plan. He agreed and painfully explained to Maddalena that he would come back later when he was able.

With their departure, Maddalena's world shrank back to the dryness of her life. Cristoforo had been an oasis, even though they had little time together the whole year he was there. She had become attached to Liliana as she had nursed the two babies. Even though Cristoforo assured her he would come back, Maddalena felt that, being with his new family back in Italy, he probably might not. Maddalena had no time to mourn. Running the store became more and more of a burden to her as Massimo became less and less involved in the store and with the children. His anger constantly exploded into rages, yelling at her and her children for making his life miserable. When he stormed out of the store, she was left to manage the five children and the counter. Zi' Angelino and Zi' Enrico tried to talk to him, but their admonitions fell on deaf ears. Massimo was untouched, unmoved, and unseeing.

The day Felicetta and Assunta visited Maddalena and found she was pregnant again they feared she would break under the new pressures. Assunta offered a solution.

"Why don't I remind him of that house on my street that I told him about? It is large enough for all the children, has an extra basement flat, and an attic. The children can go out to play on the street with the other children and besides, Maddalena, I would be only half a block down the street from you and could see you often."

Maddalena's heart warmed at the thought of being close to Assunta, but the warmth immediately was chilled as she remembered Massimo's usual off-hand rejection of anything he himself had not thought of.

"He'll never do it if you suggest it, Assunta," she said quietly and regretfully.

"That's easy," Felicetta rushed in, excited to have found a solution, "next time we visit we'll bring Paolo along and let <u>him</u> talk about it. If that doesn't work, nothing will. I'm sure he'll listen to Paolo."

They bided their time, and in the late fall of 1921 they made the momentous visit. Paolo, in his gentle, tactful way, offered Massimo a way out of his tormented life.

"You could sell your inventory and buy this house. Then you would be in a bigger place, find an easier job and the children would be out of your way."

Massimo jumped at the idea. Sell the inventory? Get away from the detested counter he was chained to? Freedom to move? An easier job? The answer to all these questions was, "Yes, yes, yes."

"Paolo," he practically shouted as he jumped up, "that is exactly what I need to do. This business is not for me."

Maddalena, Felicetta, and Assunta looked at each other with as little expression as possible, hiding their elation for fear he would change his mind. Paolo promised to bring some friends to help with the move. Massimo immediately put up a sign on the store window, "Inventory for Sale." In a few weeks a deal was made with one of their customers. Before the end of the year they moved into 2104 Kendall Street.

Chapter Nineteen

Anna Felice shifted restlessly in her seat. When the conductor called out, "Chicago, next stop!" she reorganized her baggage, settled back in her seat and gave in to her thoughts. What would it be like? This was her first visit to her brother Massimo since they left Italy more than 10 years ago. They had taken different paths—she to Pennsylvania, he to Chicago. She had been very angry when she was forced to marry Attilio, an older man from the village. But she was grateful that he had brought her to America. She remembered life in the boarding house where she and Attilio stayed when they first arrived in Pennsylvania. She had been surrounded by uprooted, lonely men, some rough and loud. Dogged by the persistent amorous attempts of Attilio, she sank into a despair that overshadowed her cold anger. At sixteen, tall and graceful with beautiful brown hair and hazel eyes, Anna Felice sent out an off-putting aura of disdain to the men around her. In spite of this, they could not help but look at her with hungry eyes. But with her ever-present doting husband, no men would dare approach her.

Then it happened. Everyone talked about a new boarder coming that evening. She yawned and felt a twitch of disgust. "Yet another one," she thought as she walked from the kitchen to the dining area.

She was expected to help serve and was happy to be busy and occupied. That evening, as she finished setting the plates on the table, she turned to go back to the kitchen. The new boarder walked in, smiled and said *"Buona sera,"* in a gentle voice. Her heart leaped into her throat, choking off her breath. A cold shiver ran through her, and she rushed back to the kitchen in silence with lowered eyes. Once in the kitchen, she tried to pull herself together, but nothing could stop the inner storm.

When she had to start serving the men, she caught another glimpse of the newcomer out of the corner of her eye. Although he was seated, she remembered he was tall. Now she saw auburn hair, blue eyes, a quick smile, and pleasant features. Later she heard he was nineteen years old and his name was Innocenzo Manzali. She was smitten.

As the weeks passed, he became part of the household. When Attilio was not around, Innocenzo held her with his eyes and she realized he too was smitten. It was an impossible situation. Yet over time, there was an unspoken declaration between them that they wanted to be together. They began to find ways to talk to each other when no one was around.

Knowing that Attilio could possibly find a job somewhere else and that Anna Felice would have to move with him, they decided to act quickly, and frantically made a plan. He would buy two tickets to the furthermost town at the opposite end of Pennsylvania. They would leave when the men were at work, walking out with only the clothes on their backs and whatever money Innocenzo had saved. They would go to the train station separately, waiting until just before the train left to avoid people seeing them standing around. On the train, they would sit apart as far from each other as possible and re-unite in the new town. A daring plan and it worked.

The next day they found themselves in New Castle, Pennsylvania, a mining town where Innocenzo went to work in the coal mines, now going by the name Jim Manzali. When he was injured at work, they moved to Oakfield, New York, a small railroad town. There they bought and ran a highly successful Italian restaurant with rooms on the second floor to rent to Italian men recently arrived in America. Next door to the restaurant was their two-storied family home with a porch circling around the front and the side. Behind the buildings, an orchard and garden gave them fresh fruit and vegetables for their own use and for the restaurant. The villagers and boarders knew that at Anna's restaurant they would eat very well. She sighed with deep satisfaction at her accomplishments. She knew that it was her strength and organizational ability that had moved everything forward. Jim was gentle and kind—she smiled at the thought of their first years together—but he had little initiative to start things. Yet he never got in her way, and he helped wherever he could.

An unspoken sadness had clouded their days, however, because after many years together, they had never been able to have children. Anna Felice knew that Massimo and Maddalena had six children, had lost one, and that another was on the way. It irked her that the quiet shy girl she had once offered life lessons to in the piazza turned out to have a fruitful motherhood, while she, Anna Felice, was barren. Her lips tightened and she drew herself in. The satisfaction of all her accomplishments could not cover her bitter loss.

She did not look forward to this visit. Although she and Jim were very well situated in Oakfield, they considered a possible move to California to avoid the harsh winters—thus a stop-over in Chicago was almost obligatory. She had no desire to see her brother. They had nothing in common. She set goals and saw them through. He did nothing but cause trouble. She gritted her teeth as she thought of the constant turmoil in their home in Sella di Corno. During his rages, she and Bettina had to cower in a safe corner of the house until his anger was spent. Her parents were at a loss as to how to control his behavior. They had been so happy when the Ferraras had offered their daughter, Maddalena, to him in marriage. Maybe, they thought, this would calm him down. They knew the villagers were horrified at the marriage. Everyone was relieved when he left for America—everyone except Maddalena. Now the burden was hers to carry the rest of her life. For a moment, Anna Felice felt sorry for her. However, the moment passed quickly as she thought of all those children.

A violent jerk of the train's brakes brought her back. Soon she would face him. The passengers were hurriedly filling the aisles and grabbing their suitcases. She joined them. No time to dread the situation, no way to run away from it. When she stepped off the train onto the platform, there he was—handsome as ever, lean, medium height, and dead eyes. He had changed very little. *"Buon giorno,"* she called out. He came toward her, answering *"Buon giorno"* in a flat voice and took her suitcase. Without another word he started for the station. She tried to keep up with him as he impatiently moved through the crowd, into the station and finally to the streetcar. Once they were seated, she started the conversation asking how everyone was, particularly, Maddalena. He answered, offering no details, that everyone was fine, and soon a silence fell between them.

She turned her attention to her surroundings. Having lived always in small towns, she was captivated by the myriad sights, sounds, and energy of the city. Riding the streetcar itself was a new experience. Everyone walked in Oakfield. The noise the street car made, shrieking as the car curved around corners, the constant clanging of money falling into its receptacle, the calling off by the conductor of the street names at each corner, put her on edge. Added to this, the other street noises created a cacophony that grew irritating to her. The peaceful quiet of her small town came back to her, and she wished she had not come. Massimo, on the other hand, simply looked, emptily, seemingly without thought.

Soon they transferred to another streetcar, which would bring them to their destination. It would take them to Roosevelt Road, a broad street with lanes for cars in the middle, and lanes for streetcars on opposite sides. They would finally get off in front of a classic Gothic cathedral, a Catholic church called Saint Charles Borromeo. It was the center of a cluster of huge gray stone buildings including the priest's house, an elementary school, and the nuns' quarters. The nuns were the Sisters of Charity of the Blessed Virgin Mary, a teaching order that ran the elementary school. A beautiful garden separated the church from the priest's house. Anna Felice was impressed by the size and organization of the complex. As they walked down the street, another large three-storied brick building came into view on the corner of the next block. This was an extension of the complex, the high school with the same order of nuns where the children would complete their Catholic education. Anna Felice also found it impressive with its red brick classical lines.

As they continued their walk down Hoyne Avenue, the world of the neighborhood came alive. In front of small cottages on either side of the street, people were sitting on stoops or backless chairs visiting and enjoying the September Indian Summer of Chicago, the summer one did not expect. This was not the choking twenty-four hour heat of July and August, but a gentle heat with cooler evenings.

It was late afternoon and the screams of children at play rang around her. Once they crossed Taylor Street, Massimo muttered, "We're almost there." Several moments later, they turned off Hoyne Avenue onto a large, empty wedge-shaped lot where children were playing baseball. There were two cottages at the wide end of the lot, one facing Hoyne Avenue and the other Kendall Street. The lot gradually became narrower until it ended at the point where the two streets intersected. It served as the recreation center for the neighborhood. The children refitted their baseball game so that the bases were in the form of a triangle instead of the usual diamond. Also, on this lot, the entire community enjoyed the *festas* which occurred twice a year to commemorate the patron saint of their villages back home.

As they walked along on the wide end of the lot, avoiding the catcher and batter at their game, Massimo pointed to a dark gray cottage on the opposite side of the street facing the lot. The house had a basement flat, an upstairs flat, and an attic. A long row of stairs led to the upper flat. On the left was a three-storied red brick apartment building and on the right, a one story cottage. This was 2104 Kendall Street, the home they had recently moved into.

As they waited to cross the street, Anna Felice was struck by the number of children playing on the streets and sidewalks. They were everywhere, playing 'kick the can,' 'hopscotch,' and 'pinners.' They made it hard to get through. In addition to the children, she had never seen so many adults idly sitting and visiting on their stoops or on chairs brought outside, as they enjoyed the cooler fall weather—that blessed transition from steamy summer to bitter winter.

As they stepped off the curb, a little boy's voice called out, "Hi, Pa." Massimo grunted a curt, "Oh" in response. When Anna Felice asked who he was, Massimo answered in Italian, "That's Andy, one of my kids. He's crazy about baseball."

She looked into the child's upturned eleven-year-old face and saw the hazel eyes and handsome features of his father. The face was dirty and his hair was uncombed. She tightened up and pursed her lips. Cleanliness was a passion with her. She thought, "How could Maddalena let her child run around like that? What kind of a mother is she?" They started to cross the street, dodging the children running in every direction. They did not see Maddalena peering out of the living room window, which faced the empty lot.

Chapter Twenty

Maddalena watched them as they approach the house. The tall erect figure, neatly dressed with her hat firmly placed on her head, brought back unpleasant memories. She panicked. It was clear to her. The overbearing childhood mentor who had condescendingly opened up the facts of life to her would now find plenty to criticize her for. She gripped the one-year-old Clara to her and rushed to the back of the flat. Longing to run out the door and be gone forever, she set Clara down on the kitchen floor and tightened the dishtowel she had wrapped around her head.

Severe headaches plagued her after she was released from the hospital … the hospital … the horror of it all. Angelina, now four, tugged at her skirts. Giving her a cookie to quiet her, Maddalena tried not to think of it all, but the dreadful memory had seeped into her body, her thoughts and her spirit. She felt devastated. It came at her wherever she turned. She had been so desperate: six children to feed, clothe, and care for, and with no money. Occasionally, a large box for the poor filled with canned goods would come from a church organization, supplementing their government relief. Maddalena was exhausted all the time and barely could bend over the bathtub with the scrub board to wash their clothes and then hang them out on the back porch to dry. The relentless day-to-day demands were draining her completely. Massimo raged at her more often and began to threaten her. "Some-a day-a, some-a day-a, a-ma gonna kill-a you!" he yelled. It began to be his theme.

When she found she was pregnant again, she sat and wept, alone, in despair. Then she remembered the neighborhood women's talk of how they successfully self-aborted. She shrank in horror at the thought of it, but it pursued her. Could she? Would she? No! She loved her children deeply; they were the joy of her life, and she would love this one too, but, her nerves were shattered. She couldn't go on with never a moment's rest. Never a moment free of the anxiety for their welfare. Never a moment free of Massimo's whims that conceived them and then abandoned them at their birth. They were bred with indifference followed by total detachment. All the responsibilities became hers. No, she could not go on like this.

Finally, after days of turmoil, she knew she could not wait much longer. Felicetta and Assunta had begged her not to do it, but she had already decided. She planned it well: the older children would be in school; Massimo would be gone; and Silia would take Angelina and Clara to visit Assunta who lived on the lower end of Kendall Street. When it was all clear, she would do it quickly.

She had felt the hard floor under her body as she lay spread-eagle with the coat hanger in her right hand. A moment of fear and hesitation stayed her hand. Then she felt a sharp pain as the cold metal moved through the soft tissue of her vagina. There was no turning back, and she forced it to go all the way.

At midnight she awoke with a raging fever and a severe headache. Her moaning disturbed Massimo, who grumbled, "Go back to sleep!" By morning she was unable to get out of bed. Her right arm was so swollen she was unable to lift it. She sent Silia to get Assunta, who then immediately sent for Felicetta. They both feared for Maddalena's life. They knew what she had done. By the time Felicetta arrived, an ambulance and a large crowd of people were gathered in front of the house to take her to the hospital.

When Felicetta went inside, she found neighbors milling around, the children with fear-filled faces standing quietly in shock, and

Massimo helplessly viewing the situation. Quickly she and Assunta agreed to take the two youngest children home with them. Massimo would have to deal with the others.

Felicetta noticed Angelina pressing against the door jamb as they carried Maddalena out of the house. She bent down and whispered into Angelina's ear, "You're coming to visit me at my house for awhile." The four-year-old looked up at her adoringly. She loved Felicetta. She was always warm and kind, and Angelina loved going to her house to visit. It was so different from her own house; it felt orderly and quiet, and she loved to run to the kitchen at the end of the flat when the elevated train rumbled past. A sudden fear crossed her mind that she might wet the bed, and Felicetta would send her away. But the moment passed and, distracted from her mother's dilemma, she took Felicetta's hand and was ready to go. Maddalena had seen none of this. The pain had been all consuming.

A rattling at the front door and loud voices brought her back to the present. The dreaded moment was here. She had to face it. Anna Felice had arrived.

She walked from the kitchen to the living room to meet them. Anna Felice quickly scrutinized Maddalena. "She's a mess," she thought. Wisps of hair slipped through the towel around her head, and a formless house dress hung loosely on her rounded body. One child was in her arms, another hanging onto her dress, and the thirteen-year-old Silia in the background. The three boys were all out in the street.

Maddalena's face was pale, drawn and pinched. When she spoke, her voice was so weak that Anna Felice had to strain to hear it. "*Come stai?*" (how are you?), Maddalena asked.

"*Bene,*" answered Anna Felice, and she went on to describe in detail the train ride and the streetcar ride, complaining about the noise and the irritating people, and the taciturn Massimo who had already disappeared.

Maddalena drew her to the kitchen to offer her a sandwich since it was past dinnertime. It was now sundown, and the voices of the neighborhood mothers calling their children home drifted into the house. "Al-beh-eh-eh-rto, Gio-vah-vah-ah-nee," they sang in long drawn out sounds. Their calls triggered Maddalena. *"Scusi"* (excuse me) she said as she went quickly to the front door and added her calls, "An-dray-ay-ay-yah, En-ree-ree-ree-cco, Fran-chay-ay-ay-sco." The children hardly responded. The dark was too delicious. Later the mothers' voices changed to crisp, short, threat-laden sounds—"Al-beh-rto—Gio-vah-nee." At the new tone of voice the streets began to empty out as the children reluctantly dragged themselves home.

Anna Felice sat in disbelief, her half-eaten sandwich resting on the plate, as the three boys came storming into the house, filling it with turmoil as they stomped around, pushing and shoving and bickering. Disgusted with the lack of discipline, their unruliness, and the chaos, she gave up even trying to carry on a conversation.

As Maddalena prepared the children for bed, Anna Felice walked to the front of the flat and stepped out the front door. The air in the basement flat was dank and damp. She needed to breathe fresh air. The flat was below street level. A small patch of hard dirt and weeds led to a concrete wall connecting with three horizontal iron railings set at the sidewalk level. Some men were sitting on the top rail, their feet hooked into the bottom one. They were talking in loud voices, sometimes in argumentative, angry tones. She could hear a low buzz of the women's voices, still seated outdoors, enjoying the cool evening. "Why don't they go back into their houses?" she thought impatiently. She had never known or suffered a steamy, unbearable Chicago summer.

She turned to go back into the flat and looked around her. The living room was a large extended space with no windows and a pot bellied coal stove for heat at the far end. The darkness was depressing. Opposite the room were two bedrooms, each with a window facing a walkway going the extent of the house from front to back. She noticed the sparseness of furniture—bedrooms with no dressers, only chairs holding piles of clothing. The bathroom, close to the kitchen, had barely enough room to move. The bathtub was filled with clothes soaking to be washed at some time later, the scrub board lying idly in their midst. Across from the bathroom was a small room containing a stairway that ended in a trap-door. It pushed upward and emptied into the upstairs kitchen. Off the kitchen was another bedroom and a doorway leading to a large storage room. From the storage room, a door opened up into a dirt wine cellar where Massimo had three large wooden casks of homemade wine.

Maddalena called Anna Felice to have a cup of coffee, and the sudden quiet in the house settled around the two of them. Maddalena asked about Jim and the restaurant. As they sat visiting, Anna Felice shrank in horror as she watched a huge black rat walk along the pipe that ran across the length of the kitchen just below the ceiling. "*Madonna mia*," she exclaimed. "*Una zocola!*" (a rat).

Maddalena with great embarrassment answered, "Unfortunately, they're all over. I'm sorry."

They had little to say to each other. Finally, Maddalena showed her to her bedroom, a tiny room next to the kitchen, and they said goodnight. Massimo still had not appeared. Once Anna Felice was settled in her bed, she decided to get a glass of water. She walked into the kitchen and turned on the light. She stepped back and froze. The floor was swarming with cockroaches. Giving up the idea of getting water, she rushed back to her room and once again crawled into bed.

"What have I gotten myself into?" she thought. "Maddalena is a mess. The house is disorderly, the children are disorderly, and now this." Anna Felice mused on the situation, feeling restless, unable to sleep. Then the quiet was broken. She could hear squeaky sounds and scurrying feet in the walls of her bedroom. She shrank in horror. More rats! There would be no sleep for her tonight. It was all too much. She wanted to be back in her well-ordered, spotless house. Yes! She would leave tomorrow and not spend another night in this hellhole. She would give up the idea of California for another time.

The next morning she informed Massimo that he had to take her back to the train station. After saying good-bye to Maddalena, her parting remark was, "You have so many children, why don't you let me have one of them?" Then, eyeing the small four-year-old, shyly peeking out from behind her mother's skirt, she said, "*Quella*" (that one).

Chapter Twenty-One

Three years later, Maddalena sat in her train seat bound for Oakfield, New York. With her were Angelina now seven, and Clara, four years of age. Anna Felice's *quella* had stuck in Maddalena's mind and sounded over and over again. It came back to her when Frankie had to be rushed to Cook County Hospital after having convulsions and she was told he was suffering from malnutrition. "Just take him home and feed him," they said. They wanted to keep him a few days to restore him but after she was alone with him, she feared that they might take him from her for good. She dressed him quickly and sneaked out of the hospital.

The *quella* came back to her again when Enrico got tangled at her feet, and she knocked over a kettle of boiling spaghetti water onto his shoulder and back. Again, the county hospital had to treat him for days with severe burns that would scar him permanently. She spent as much time at the hospital as she could, while Assunta tended the other children. Maddalena worried constantly and feared the authorities might take her children from her. It ate at her soul to see her children suffer from lack of food, to see them barely clothed against the bitter Chicago winter.

The one bright spot was the aftermath of Andrew's bout with diphtheria. Because of his chronic lung problem, the county set him up to attend a special school called 'The Sunshine School,' where he was provided lunch, naps, and outdoor exercise. She was also told to take him to Lincoln Park once a week on Sundays. That meant a streetcar ride that cost seven cents for her and three cents for him. Finding a way to get the money was always a pressure on her, but she managed to do it for her son's health. Her children were her life, and she would do anything to help them. It was all of these struggles that had led her to this train ride.

The *quella* had persisted in her mind to the point that she decided she must give Angelina this chance at a better life. With Anna Felice she would have plenty of food and warm clothing, with the kindly Jim to temper Anna Felice's cold, rigid nature. Angelina was quiet and compliant and would be no trouble for Anna Felice. To lose Angelina would be painful, but she would do it temporarily and come back for her later.

She looked down at the seat next to her and found that the children were not there. For a moment she panicked, then realized they could not have gone far. She discovered them at the end of the car, where strangers were playing with them. After feeding them the lunch she had prepared, she covered them with a blanket, and stroking their backs, got them to sleep. Her thoughts turned to Cristoforo. He had stayed with them the last summer to earn money to bring his family back to America. Jobs were scarce in Italy. After a summer's hard work he returned to Italy and assured Maddalena he would be back, with his family, to stay permanently. In the meantime, Massimo's younger brother Giulio came and stayed with them. The two brothers, with their similar temperaments, could hardly tolerate each other, and eventually Giulio went to live with Anna Felice. With all this going on, Maddalena had taken in a boarder to earn some money. Serafino was newly arrived in America and was grateful for a room and food. His payments made her trips to Lincoln Park possible.

During Massimo's recent drinking bouts, he was particularly hostile. In desperation Maddalena tried to find a way out. She had heard that a judge in the downtown Chicago courthouse would take a mother and children and find a new home for them if they were in danger. One evening, after another drunken rage had terrorized her, she decided that the judge was the only way out. The next morning, she gathered all the children around her and walked to the streetcar stop. She wasn't sure where the judge would be, but when the streetcar ended in the downtown area she would ask.

While they waited, Assunta came by, and in shock, she asked, "Maddalena, where are you going with all your children?" When her plan was divulged, Assunta sadly pointed out to her, "But Maddalena, it's not a good idea. They might separate the children from you and put them in different homes. Please don't do this. You might lose your children. Come, let's go home."

As they crossed Taylor Street and the empty lot back to the basement flat on Kendall Street, Maddalena felt that her last hope was gone.

Oakfield, New York, was a small railroad town, and Anna's Restaurant, as it was known, had a reputation for authentic, fresh Italian food. The railroad men flocked to it, as did the townspeople. Maddalena looked around her; seeing the thriving restaurant, the comfortable family home next door, and the beautiful orchard and garden in the rear, she was amazed at what Anna Felice had created. She was grateful that Angelina would be part of it all, but the thought of leaving her daughter behind almost broke her heart. She could only stay overnight and as she fell asleep in the comfortable bed, wrapped in the cleanliness and warmth of her room, she hardly had time to contrast this one night with what she would soon return to at home.

The next morning, as Maddalena prepared to leave the house for the train station with Jim, she looked at the child she was leaving behind and felt the sting of separation. At the same time, a wave of remorse swept over her as she recalled the hot stove incident. Someone had given Angelina a toy flatiron when she was three years old. Having watched Maddalena place the big flatiron on the kitchen stove and then iron the clothes, she knew that the iron was supposed be hot, so she had pulled up a chair to the pot-bellied stove and attempted to place the toy iron on the lid. When the chair slipped, she fell and banged her head against the stove as she went down. Her cries of pain brought Maddalena, who found her with blood spattered over her right temple. In her fear and frustration, Maddalena had struck her—a slap on the back—and after treating the wound, had angrily yanked her off to her bed.

Angelina would bear a scar on her temple, but Maddalena would always feel the scar of regret and shame over losing control with her helpless child. And now nothing could assuage the grief she felt as the car pulled away and she waved goodbye. The memory and the moment tore at her heart. She tightened her hold on the four-year-old Clara, as she watched Angelina's small figure standing next to Anna Felice's tall one recede into the distance.

Chapter Twenty-Two

Marino, Italy
1927

Cristoforo sat in the piazza. All around him the piazza throbbed with life. He, however, sat in an icy fury, shut off from everything around him. He looked at the people, but did not see them. The twittering of the birds and the cooing of the doves fell on deaf ears. The warmth of the Italian sun caressed his shoulders, but he felt nothing, nothing except the cold anger that chilled his blood and dulled his senses. He would not confront her. No, he had already accepted as the truth the innuendos and veiled remarks about his wife Elena's possible indiscretions while he was in America. The depth of his anger resonated with a dim remembrance of a past betrayal that had destroyed all reason—the five-year-old, abandoned by his mother. He would never forgive Elena. Cutting her off without a word, he would book passage back to America.

The fragrant smell of coffee from a nearby bar drew him out of his immobile state and, after downing the strong cup, he felt the need to walk. The narrow winding streets of the village pulled him forward. He had always loved Marino—discovering it when he first visited Elena's family. He had happily left Sella di Corno to move there, though he would have inherited the family business, had he remained at home.

121

But he had wanted no part of it, or of the village where he had grown up.

Marino was one of a group of villages southeast of Rome that was called the Castelli Romani. These villages were scattered at the foot of the Alban Hills and served as a day trip for Romans to get away from the city for fresh air, good food, and wine. Cristoforo had always enjoyed the peaceful lifestyle, the local food, and the rhythm of the evenings in the piazza—but there had been no work. Since work was always available in the growing city of Chicago, he had begun using his visits to Maddalena as opportunities to earn money. Finally, after going back and forth a few times, he had decided to move his family permanently to Chicago. Now that was not going to happen. Again the anger surged in him, causing his walking to become more rapid as he pounded the stones under his feet.

His thoughts turned to his children. He loved his children. Mercedes was five years old and Liliana, seven. Mercedes was too young, but Liliana could possibly go back with him. Maddalena would welcome her. Had she not nursed her as an infant along with Angelina? He would talk to Liliana and offer her the chance. His attitude toward children was that they must be totally controlled, and must submit to a discipline that would break their unruly spirit and conform to the image that he required. Children who did not work did not eat. However, he would not go to the extreme of Nonna Amelia. Her clear words rang in his memory, "Children must be kept a little bit hungry to learn what hunger is." That far he would not go. He wanted Liliana with him. He could not force her, but he would make a strong push for it.

With his decision made, he looked around and found himself on a rise at the outskirts of the village. The day had passed him by, and he realized that night had fallen. His gaze swept over the darkened Alban hills and he saw, nestled in their folds, the shining, sparkling lights of the scattered villages scintillating with the brightness of diamonds. They twinkled like an inverted night sky. For the moment, he caught his breath at the beauty of the scene lying in the distance. He sighed as he realized that this would be the last time he would see this view. He would leave for Rome the next day.

The following day he took Liliana aside and told her she must choose—either to go back to America with him or stay with her mother. He would not return. Liliana tearfully chose her mother. There was nothing he could say that would change her mind.

He boarded a ship leaving Naples for America. His fury was barely spent by the time he reached Ellis Island. During the train ride to Chicago, he thought about his two daughters, but his rage overshadowed his love for them. He vowed he would never trust another woman, and instead, he would give himself over to protecting Maddalena. Only she could be trusted.

Chapter Twenty-Three

Kendall Street and the streets that bordered it were crawling with children. School was out and kids of all ages made the streets their playground. Everywhere one looked, like busy little bees—they played in the empty lot, on the streets, and on the sidewalks.

The streets rang with the cries of, "ahlee, ahlee, auction free, free" as 'hide and seek' reached its peak of excitement when the 'seeker' discovered the 'hider'. At that cry, the players leaped out from their hiding places, shrieking and screaming as they rushed back to the central location to begin the game all over again with the discovered one now 'it'. The excitement of finding a good spot to hide in, and the fear of being discovered, gave the thrills and chills that kept the game alive.

Others played 'kick the can', hurtling themselves in every direction to kick into the goal. On the sidewalks, they played the quieter game of 'pinners' by throwing a small ball against the rim of the red bricks of the tenement building. If it came back without bouncing on the sidewalk, a point was gained. Some played 'hopscotch', the chalk figures fading from use, or 'ball and jacks', where they sat on the curb and scooped up the metal jacks as the ball rose and fell.

The older teenage boys gathered at the corner where Kendall Street joined Taylor and Almond Streets for their crap games. They chose the corner so that their lookout could watch in all directions for the police; shooting dice for money was considered gambling, which was illegal. When the lookout shouted, "Chees it, the cops," the dice magically disappeared as quickly as the boys dispersed. The police never had a chance to come upon them.

Occasionally, the street players had to make way for a horse-drawn wagon selling ice. The ice-man called out his wares to the women inside their homes. As the women appeared at their doors, or at their windows in the upper story flats, giving him their order, the children clustered around the wagon, waiting for the ice-man to clamp the huge block of ice securely with his giant tongs and lift it off the wagon to be delivered and placed inside the ice box. The minute he walked away they dived into the wagon to snatch fresh chips of ice to suck on in the summer heat. Nor did they mind interrupting their play at the welcome song of the watermelon man. When they heard the lilting sounds "Wateemayloh …. Wateemayloh," they followed the wagon eagerly hoping to somehow obtain some of the red, cold, sweet delight. This was harder than the ice because the watermelon man did not have to leave his wagon. Their mouths watered as they watched the women convince him to plug a melon so they might taste it before they bought. Only if a melon accidentally fell and broke apart could they descend upon it and have it disappear before the watermelon man's eyes. Few of them ever had the chance to get their fill of the red, sweet fruit.

On extremely hot humid days, the city sidewalks burned. The insides of houses were insufferably hot. There was no air conditioning and there were no fans. No breeze or breath of air stirred to cause some movement. The heat sat like an unmoving, heavy, all-enveloping suffocating blanket. There was no escape, since no one had cars or the street car fare to take them to the blessed coolness of the lake or a park. The air at midnight was as hot and humid as it had been at noon. Desperately, people sat outside until the wee hours of the morning to avoid going into their 'oven-like' houses. Maddalena placed blankets on the floor of the front porch so the three girls could sleep outside, while she slept in a chair at the top of the stairs to keep watch over them.

During the day, the children found recourse from the oppressive heat in the Johnny pump, their nickname for the fire hydrant. Someone had learned how to turn it on and the children took turns running through its crashing waters to cool off. The screams and joyous howls of the children brought smiles of satisfaction to their watchful mothers. However, the police soon showed up, shooed the children off, and closed the hydrant. This interference by 'the cops' did not deter the children since no one would confess to turning on the hydrant. Waiting a reasonable time, the pump was turned on again, and the game continued.

Then the *lupini* man showed up, his cart carrying a variety of snacks for sale in small bags. The children were willing to stop their play if they, or a friend, had the coveted penny to look over the possible choices. A small bag of *lupini*, a yellow, round bean covered by a thick white skin, was a favorite. The skin was bitten into and slipped off as the released *lupini* offered moments of chewy pleasure. Another favorite were the *ceci*, salted, roasted chickpeas. In contrast to the bland *lupini*, the *ceci* were crunchy, harder to chew, and lasted longer. But, the very best were the *pinoli*, the Italian pine nuts. The outer brown hard shell had to be cracked open to reveal the sweet, white, tasty nut. The lucky buyers planted themselves on the curb or the lower steps of their houses and savored the few moments it took to empty their bags. They alternated between blissfully chewing and spitting out skins and shells onto the sidewalk or into the street. As they chomped and munched, the unfortunate, "penniless" ones, sat close to their luckier friends and hungrily eyed the delicious contents of the bags, sometimes cajoling a sample or two.

The most exciting sound that drew them from their play, however, was the hurdy-gurdy man cranking his box to produce exciting melodies. Even more than that, the antics of his monkey, dressed in his little red suit and red cap, enchanted them. In the midst of their play, whenever they heard the hurdy-gurdy man in the distance, they would drop everything and rush to meet him. When he stopped cranking out the music, whichever child thought he could, would run home to wheedle a penny out of his mother to get the music going and the monkey doing his "monkey business."

Later in the evening, after the children had been gathered in for the night, the men, having returned home from work and having eaten their dinner, would take over the empty lot for their bocce games. Then the sounds on the streets became those of the balls striking each other and the shouts of the men, ranging from declarations of success to angry arguments at failure.

As he ran the bases in his baseball game, Andy's eye caught a familiar figure coming down the street. It was a rigid figure, walking firmly with purpose. Recognizing immediately that it was Zio Cristoforo from Italy, he abandoned the game to race to his house across the street from the lot. He hurtled up the fourteen stairs that led to their upstairs flat, burst past the front door and yelled, "Ma! Ma! It's Zi' Cristoforo back from Italy! Where are you, Ma?"

He found her in the bathroom, kneeling at the tub, hands on the scrub board washing the family clothes. She leaned back, shaking her hands out and asked, "Are you sure?"

"Oh yeah," he went on breathlessly. "I know his walk. He was walking fast like he was in a hurry."

"And the children?" she asked.

"Oh, no Ma, he was alone. Well, I gotta get back to the game, Ma." And he ran back to the lot.

For a moment Maddalena was still, thinking "alone?" He was supposed to bring Elena and children back with him. Her back ached and her shoulders hurt. She looked wearily at the pail sitting on the toilet seat next to her where she had piled the wrung-out clothes waiting to be hung out to dry.

The bathroom was off the end of the kitchen. It was barely wide enough for one person to walk past the tub to get to the toilet. The washbowl was wedged in the corner between the tub and the toilet, and one had to lean over it to wash their hands and face. There were no toothbrushes so they never had to brush their teeth. Opposite the bathroom door was the trap door which opened up to stairs leading down to the basement flat. Next to the trap door at the wall in the corner was a pot-bellied coal stove that heated the kitchen. A cooking stove to the left had four openings with lids, which could be lifted off to put in coal or wood used for cooking. There was a warming space above the lids and an oven below. Next to the cooking stove, a window looked out on the neighbor's house below. The side wall contained the sink and finally a door leading outside to a partially enclosed porch used as a storage area. Stepping off the porch was an extended roof-top over Massimo's wine cellar and the downstairs storage room. It ended at a fence over which the garbage was tossed into the alley, adding to the existing pile from the previous days. This formed a huge open mass of rotting, stinking food. The alley was lined on both sides with everyone's garbage, creating a feast for the rats that infested the houses and the neighborhood. The ragman could barely guide his horse through the narrow space in the center of the alley. His call of "rags and iron" brought the women to the alley fence if they had something to sell. Being fearful of the American system, no one dared complain.

It was to this rooftop that Maddalena would carry out her pail of wet clothes to be hung on the stretched-out clothes lines. Silia helped, but the task was enormous with a boarder and a large family to be provided with clean clothes. The sheets were the hardest because they filled up the tub and were difficult to hang.

As she gingerly twisted her body in the tight space to get off her knees, she heard the front door open and Cristoforo's voice calling, "Maddalena, *dove sei?*" (where are you?)

She couldn't get to her feet fast enough. He found her half up, leaning on the rim of the tub to balance herself. He helped her up, and they went to sit at the kitchen table. His heart always ached when he looked at her. She didn't deserve this punishing life. There was never any respite for her. He was happy to be back to at least help keep a lid on Massimo's unpredictable rages. He knew that Massimo tolerated him for the money he contributed.

She broke into his thoughts and asked, "And Elena? The children?"

"It was not the right time," he curtly answered and followed immediately with, "Let me help you." Picking up the pail from the toilet seat, he felt the wet weight of it, and then noticed the tub still filled with clothes. As he carried the pail to the rooftop outside, he made up his mind that some day he would buy his dear sister a washing machine.

Chapter Twenty-Four

An invitation was extended by Anna Felice to have Ricco, age fourteen, and Frankie, age eleven, spend the summer in Oakfield. Anna Felice's experience with Angelina was working out well, and since Jim loved having children around, they urged Maddalena to send the boys. The fear Maddalena always felt when her children were out of reach wrestled with her desire to give them every opportunity. Cristoforo urged her to let them go, and she agreed reluctantly.

"I ain't gonna go," Ricco proclaimed. "I got things to do here with my friends and there ain't no way I'm leaving. Besides, I don't like Zi' Felice—she's mean." He knew she was strict, and he wanted no part of her discipline. "Let Frankie and Andy go."

Andy, age 15, quickly added his lament in a pleading voice, "Aw, come on Ma, you know I can't go. I got baseball practice all summer. That would put me way behind. I'm not leaving either."

Frankie was happy to go, but Maddalena would not let him go alone. She asked Cristoforo to intervene. He took Ricco aside. "Just think, Ricco—you will go on an exciting train ride, see a new part of the country, and have plenty to eat in the restaurant. How many of your friends get to do that, huh? When you get back, you'll have plenty to tell your friends and their eyes will pop open." The prospect of all this was appealing. Ricco liked the idea of being able to lord it over his friends, and he visualized himself holding the stage as he narrated his exciting experiences. Ricco was action oriented and puffed himself up whenever he found an audience. Failing to make it in school created a need for bravado, and the city streets called for a strong front. He would go.

Maddalena was grateful. Ricco was a great worry for her. She never knew where he was, who he was with, or what he was doing. He came and went as he pleased, cutting himself off from the family. She thought Jim would have a calming effect on him. While he was in Oakfield, her worries would be temporarily lessened.

So Ricco and Frankie would be gone the month of July and maybe August, if things went well. When Cristoforo took them to the train, Maddalena watched them cross the empty lot. Notwithstanding that the train went directly to Oakfield and the two boys would be traveling together, a nagging fear arose that they might be lost to her. When she received the letter that they had arrived safely, were having a good time, and that Angelina was happy to see her brothers, Maddalena relaxed. Her children were in good hands, learning new things. This made her happy. She wanted so much for them.

It was a hot summer. Andy threw himself into his baseball practice. Silia at seventeen, was blossoming into her womanhood, and a suitable husband was being sought for her. Clara and Caroline played together, and the house was quieter without the boys. Massimo alternated between drunken bouts after his weekend card games and days of total disengagement. He was either screaming and yelling curses at Maddalena, promising the day would come when he would kill her, or he would be gone, his whereabouts unknown. Maddalena never knew what to expect. Cristoforo worked.

Then a telegram came from Oakfield. There had been an accident. Ricco was safe, but Frankie was in the hospital with an eye injury. Someone needed to come and take the boys home. Maddalena's heart sank. Her knees became weak. Remembering her past fear, she felt guilty about having let them go. She knew she must be the one to bring them back. Cristoforo was working, and Massimo refused to go. Maddalena again relied on Assunta and Felicetta to take the children while she made the trip. Her anxiety during the train ride kept her from eating or sleeping.

Although Maddalena's heart swelled to see Angelina healthy and so well-dressed, she worried because she was also shy and withdrawn. Ricco looked scared, morose, and tight-lipped. The household was an emotional earthquake. Even the gentle Jim was bristling with anger, and Anna Felice could hardly contain herself.

"He smashed my car—he wrecked my car!" Jim stormed.

"That boy will come to no good!" Anna Felice ranted.

"You owe us money to buy a new car!" added Jim in a furious voice.

Maddalena helplessly waited for them to vent their full anger, observing Ricco hanging back in the corner of the room, looking frightened and contrite. Frankie was still in the hospital, but would be released the next day. Surgeons had to remove his right eye.

When the yelling subsided, the story came out that three nights earlier Ricco had taken the car for a ride with Frankie in the passenger seat. Regardless of the fact that he did not know how to drive, and obviously without Anna Felice's or Jim's permission, he had managed to start the engine and roll the car out of the garage onto the street. It was a rainy night, and the car was almost immediately out of control. Within a few hundred feet they ran into a tree. Frankie's head shot through the windshield and glass penetrated his eye. In a panic, Ricco tried to pull out the pieces of glass that protruded from his brother's eye. The crash awakened the neighborhood and very quickly the police showed up.

"We should have let the police take him!" Anna Felice screamed at Maddalena. "He's a bad boy." However, she and Jim did not charge Ricco and eventually put their concerns on the innocent victim of the situation. From then on and into his adult life, Frankie would always have a soft spot in their hearts.

Maddalena could only say, *"Mi dispiace"* (I'm sorry). "Now I want to see my son."

After Jim took Maddalena to the hospital, Anna Felice turned her attention to Angelina, who was in a state of terror at all the verbal violence that had gone on. "Now to bed," Anna Felice said as she took the child's hand to lead her to her room.

But there was no sleep for Angelina. Their angry voices rang in her ears. She sucked her right thumb furiously and rubbed her left ear lobe to pacify her anxiety. Anna Felice had tried to break her of the habit by putting pepper on the thumb and wrapping it with a cloth. But this night, she had been too overwrought to notice. It took a long time for the chaos and fear to clear, but eventually Angelina slept.

The next day, Maddalena took her two boys home. She hardly had a chance to notice the little nine-year-old girl who was looking so sadly at her mother, who was leaving her yet again. Angelina longed to go home with her too.

Chapter Twenty-Five

Life changed drastically for Angelina when Anna Felice and Jim gave up the restaurant and bought a pig farm just outside of town. School was now a two-mile walk to a two-room schoolhouse. The American way of life was opened up to her when she went to pick up a neighbor girl, Susan, to walk to school together. At Susan's house she first saw the "red stuff that jiggled in the glass." It was called "Jello." But Angelina's life-changing event was Susan's piano. When Susan taught Angelina a short little ditty, Angelina felt the world had come alive. It made music! At that moment a fire was started inside Angelina. She fell in love with the piano.

However, the thorn in Angelina's heart continued to ache. . .she wanted her mother. Earlier she had forgotten her mother's face, and when she saw her again, the sweetness and warmth were a contrast to Anna Felice's coldness and harshness. One day when they had chicken for dinner, Angelina decided to act. She took the wishbone, made her wish, broke it, carefully washed and dried it and then hid it behind the special cups that were rarely used. The ache was changed to hope.

Angelina's hope was Maddalena's desire. Maddalena sat across the kitchen table from Cristoforo and bemoaned the fact that she wanted her little daughter back. It had been four years and Anna Felice was making it very difficult.

"You know, Cristoforo, when I went two years ago to bring her home, Anna Felice screamed and yelled and practically tore her hair out at the idea. She finally asked Angelina if she liked it there and wanted to stay. When Angelina said, 'yes,' Anna Felice said 'see?' What could I do? The child looked healthy, had plenty of food, and was well dressed—so I thought, 'I'll let her stay if she's happy.' But now, it's been too long and I miss her too much. I want her home."

Cristoforo broke in and said, "I'll take off work and go and get her. Anna Felice can't push me around. I have the truck and I'll just drive there and bring her home. Anna Felice can't stop me, and this time we're not going to ask Angelina if she wants to stay. She's coming home."

Maddalena gave a sigh of relief. She knew Cristoforo's determination and his ability to stand up to Anna Felice. She missed the quiet little Angelina who, by now, was eleven years old. She mused at what changes might have taken place since she saw her last. Maddalena's endless pregnancies had kept her so busy that she had had no time to dwell on it. Now the boys were older, Clara was eight and Caroline five, so she was freer to think about her missing child.

"You know, Cristoforo," she broke into his thoughts, "Liliana would be the same age as Angelina."

Cristoforo stiffened and made no comment. Maddalena continued into the silence. "Now that Anna Felice and Jim have moved from Oakfield to the pig farm, he is probably much busier taking care of the animals. Angelina has to go much further to a country school. Thank God she has a little neighbor girl to walk the two miles with her."

At the end of the school year, Cristoforo left to bring Angelina home. He drove a rickety old truck and Maddalena worried about him making the thousand-mile trip. He wanted to leave very early in the morning to get out of the city. She handed him the packages containing his favorite sandwiches of sausage and peppers on the thick crusty bread she baked in the neighborhood communal bakery. Since so many loaves were needed to feed their large families, the women brought their dough to the bakery. There they socialized as they kneaded and shaped the dough into various sizes, long plain loaves, braided loaves and sometimes large, round ones. The loaves were then placed in the huge ovens. Some women waited for the bread, others returned home, sending their older children later to pick up the bread. It was a common sight to see a child carrying two or three huge loaves of the fragrant, recently out-of-the-oven brown crusty bread.

Cristoforo thanked her for the food and said, "Don't worry. Everything will be all right." But as he pulled away from the curb, Maddalena began her vigil of worry. She would not breathe easily until she saw him again, safe and sound, with her little girl beside him.

As she turned to go into the house, a sleeping Massimo cursed at being awakened. When she told him that Cristoforo had just left to pick up Angelina, he swore, "Cretino! (idiot), he doesn't have to wake everyone up to do it!" and went back to sleep.

On a rainy night, Cristoforo arrived at the farm. Anna Felice and Jim heard the sound of the noisy truck pulling into the driveway. When Anna Felice answered the door, she was shocked to see Cristoforo.

"What are you doing here?" she exclaimed.

He lost no time to bluntly state, "I have come to take Angelina home."

She was not happy to see him, for more than just the reason of Angelina going home. They were not on good terms due to a failed business venture they had shared. They had little to say to each other. Jim, however, was cordial and tried to make Cristoforo comfortable. The next morning, the two men walked around the farm while Anna Felice put Angelina's belongings together. By midday, the truck, with driver and young passenger sitting next to him in the cab, sputtered out of the driveway onto the highway.

Angelina did not know the man next to her except that Anna Felice told her he was her uncle and would be taking her home. She glanced over at him and saw a stern face concentrating on his driving. But after awhile, he began to sing Italian songs, one after another and then started all over repeating the same songs he had just sung.

Sometimes while he was singing, he looked over at her with a little smile. Any fear she had was dispelled, and she began to focus on trying to remember her mother's face. A happiness spread over her like the sun suddenly coming out from behind a cloud, surrounding her with its warmth. The next time he smiled at her, she smiled back. She was going home, and this man, who sang constantly with so much love for the country he had left behind, was her uncle. He was the fulfillment of the wishbone she had scrubbed clean and hidden in the cupboard months ago, wishing that she might go home.

He drove all night, stopping only briefly to snatch some sleep by the roadside. The next day the singing continued. "*Vicino mare, facciemo amore,*" he heartily rang out.

By the time they reached Chicago, she had learned some of the choruses of the songs, and she sang along with him though the words were in Italian and she had no idea what she was singing. He was delighted and smiled at her more often.

Once they entered the city, the noise, confusion, and the sheer immensity of it struck her as they made their way to the Near West Side. Oakfield and the farm were very small, quiet communities with few cars. Here, in addition to many cars, were the ear-splitting screeches of the street cars, the honking of horns and masses of people everywhere. As they pulled up in front of 2104 Kendall Street, Cristoforo turned to her and said, "This is your home."

It was late afternoon during a steamy July heat wave. The streets were jammed with children running in all directions playing their games, some dashing in and out of the water gushing from the Johnny pump. She had never seen so many children in one place. Then she saw the short, round figure with the gentle face and soft eyes come out of the house, wiping her hands on her apron, rushing to greet her. Angelina's heart felt as if it would burst with joy as Maddalena wrapped her arms around her daughter and they both cried.

"I have missed you so much," Maddalena whispered to her as she led her into the house. Cristoforo followed with her suitcases. "Clara, Caroline, come, your sister is home," Maddalena called out to the two younger girls as she went in. The girls stopped their play and followed the entourage into the house. "This is your sister," Maddalena told them. The girls stood in wonder at the well-dressed stranger and stared without comment. Angelina was quick to note their disheveled appearances and the darkness and disorder of the house.

"Come, come," Maddalena urged the weary home-comers to the kitchen, where she had prepared a fragrant, tasty lentil soup served with fresh bread. She lopped some Mazola corn oil into the soup and placed the bowls before them. Angelina smelled the savory soup, and hungrily spooned it into her mouth. Cristoforo ate with relish, dunking the bread into the soup. The younger girls, having eaten earlier, went back to their play.

Cristoforo recounted the experience with Anna Felice and the trip home. Angelina said nothing and quietly stared at Maddalena, basking in the warmth of the mother she had missed for four long years. Maddalena too, could hardly take her eyes off her daughter. She placed some special cookies she had made in front of the child and said, "*Mangia, mangia*" (eat, eat). Silia joined them and smiled warmly at her little sister. Maddalena filled a bowl with soup for Silia and continued to press Cristoforo for every detail.

When the boys came home, they regarded the newcomer curiously. Somehow Angelina looked different from any of the kids in the neighborhood. After dinner they went out for their nightly activities. Massimo was the last to appear. He glanced at her and then put his full attention on dipping his bread into the soup.

At bedtime, Maddalena, remembering that Angelina had come from having her own room, quietly explained to her that here, she would be sleeping in the same bed with her two younger sisters. Angelina said nothing; her attention was focused on the warm feelings she received from this woman who was her mother. She had so longed for it. She was home, and that was all that mattered.

Chapter Twenty-Six

Once Angelina was home and things had settled down, the attention was placed on Silia. She was quiet, made no demands, and was closely attached to her mother. She was very helpful around the house, cooking and caring for the younger children. As was the custom in their village back home, girls did not attend school. Since she had never registered, there had never been a truant officer at the door. She had a soft demeanor with soulful eyes. Later on, it was discovered that she was partially sighted.

When the topic of marriage came up, Silia diffidently confided to her mother that she liked the German fellow who ran the corner candy store. Maddalena quietly looked at her and said, "But Silia, you <u>must</u> marry an Italian." When the word got out that Silia was looking for an Italian man to marry, someone recommended Louie Rago, an Italian house painter who made good money and played the drums in a band. A deal was made, and Silia was married according to custom. The new couple moved in with the family.

Within a year, Maddalena looked forward to her first grandchild. The birth went well but the infant did not thrive, and six weeks later the baby died. Silia was devastated. Pushed into a marriage she had not welcomed, and then losing the opportunity to love her new baby, she was crushed. Maddalena also was heartbroken for her daughter, comforting her the best she could.

The customary *crepe* (a black wreath) was hung on the front door, indicating to the neighborhood that there was a death in the family. The little white coffin sat in the living room between the two windows that looked out on the empty lot across the street. For three days, friends and neighbors came and went and sat along the edges of the living room, spreading into the dining room and into the kitchen, mourning the death of the little one. After the burial, they gathered to comfort each other over roast beef sandwiches and wine and coffee. Their sadness over the life cut short melted into resignation and the acceptance that life must move on.

Louie suggested that Andy and Ricco come to work with him. He would teach them how to paint. Maddalena balked at this. She valued education passionately. Cristoforo had told her of the differences he had seen between the North and the South of Italy when he was serving in the army in the Veneto. When he saw that his fellow soldiers knew how to read, he had been inspired to teach himself.

"Now we are in America," he told her. "Schools are free and open to anyone. The boys must go to school and become whatever they choose."

His words echoed in Maddalena's heart. She saw education as a pathway to freedom from grinding poverty. But it was a battle. Education was not a primary value in the neighborhood. Most families wanted their children to go to work as soon as possible. Ricco had already given up. Andrew had been her first hope. She dreamed of his becoming a pharmacist. When she heard that Marshall High School, which served the Jewish community several miles away, was a better school than the local high school, she managed to get him in and then had to face the difficult road of raising seven cents a day to put him on a street car to get to school. Her struggle carried him through his junior year, at which time he dropped out. His persistent coughing due to chronic bronchitis and the differences in the culture isolated him from the other students. Her dream was shattered. She and Cristoforo commiserated over the loss of possibilities. Andy and Ricco would join Louie in the house painting trade.

Her next hope lay with the thirteen-year-old Frankie, who had just finished the eighth grade. He was not as tractable as Andy and, at times, was argumentative. She enrolled him in a boys' Catholic High School, hoping the discipline of the Brothers would rein him in. However, at the end of the first year, he refused to go back. Now began the frustrating game of trying to enroll him in the public school, which refused to take him without his credits from the former school. The Catholic school refused to give him his credits until his tuition was paid. There was no money to do this. After a back and forth between the two school systems, the public school expected him to repeat the ninth grade to earn the missing credits. Frankie adamantly refused and dropped out of school. Maddalena's dreams of education for her children were stymied yet again. Frankie was now on the streets, and she feared that if a truant officer caught him, he might be put into a dreaded reform school. The agony this caused her was increased by her guilt at her inability to keep the boys in at night as Cristoforo had admonished her. She felt at fault, helpless, and utterly frustrated.

Horror stories abounded of what would happen if you got picked up by the police for any little thing. The police tended to be Irish and were prejudiced against Italians. It was said that they would do anything to get a confession, even if they knew the suspect was innocent. There were stories of interrogations with bright lights blinding the suspects' eyes and painful beatings with rubber hoses. Most gruesome of all, some said the suspect would be taken to a deserted railroad yard and told he could make a run for it and escape out of town. As the suspect ran away, he would promptly be shot in the back. The police would then claim the suspect was trying to escape.

The fear of the police, however, paled in comparison to the fear of the gangs. The neighborhood was rife with them. The '42 Gang' was a loosely knit group with one center in the Halsted and Taylor area and another right down the street on Kendall and Taylor. The 'Black Hand' was a group running an overall extortion operation. When a small shop owner received a letter suggesting a protection payment, a black hand was stamped at the end of the letter as a reminder that if no payment was received, they were promised a bomb set off in their shop or an "accidental death" in the family. The shopkeeper would know better than to appeal to the police, who generally were aligned with the extortionists.

Later during her early college years, Angelina would take a job as the organist for the local Catholic church. This included playing for funerals and weddings. She used the money she earned to pay for her school expenses and to help her mother with small amounts of cash. Maddalena was delighted and proud of her daughter until one Saturday when Angelina came home and told her about the funeral she had just played for.

"What? Oh, no!" exclaimed Maddalena, jumping up from her chair and pacing the kitchen floor. Fear had turned her face pale, and she nervously faced her daughter.

"Don't worry, Ma. I only played for his funeral," Angelina assured her.

"Tell me again. What happened?" Maddalena asked, with a little shiver.

"Well," Angelina continued. "There were a lot of people in the church. When the priest gave the eulogy, he spoke very highly of the dead man. I thought it must have been someone special. After it was over, as I came out of the church, I noticed at least seven or eight open cars filled with flowers in the funeral line-up. I had never seen even one such car at other funerals. I wondered who was this famous, wonderful man that the priest spoke so highly of. I finally asked someone and he said, 'What? You don't know? That's Frank Nitti, one of Al Capone's right-hand men.'"

Angelina's recounting of the day's experience rekindled Maddalena's fear of the power and influence that the neighborhood gangs might have on her children.

No criminal activity was ever reported to the police. Even a drive-by street murder would send people scrambling into their homes to avoid being caught as witnesses. When the police arrived, there would be no one around the crime scene to be questioned. If the police knocked on adjacent doors, they were met with blank faces, people saying they saw or heard nothing. Both understood each other and the matter was closed.

One night, Maddalena was shaken out of her sleep by the sounds of blood-curdling screams. They were the screams of a woman being beaten and gang-raped in the alley just behind the back porch. Maddalena cringed in terror as she listened to the voices of men, muted and angry. She made no move to awaken Massimo, who seemed to hear nothing. There was the unwritten, unspoken law in the neighborhood that one did not interfere with gang-related activities or any crime for that matter. The personal repercussions could be worse than the crime itself.

She tossed and turned as she listened to the agonizing cries for help. It was a torment for her. Her heart ached for the poor woman, but she dared not even get out of bed or turn on a light, *"acqua in bocca"* she thought over and over again, bringing back the steadying mantra of her childhood.

As the cries diminished into pitiful whimpers, the voices of the men died down too. Finally, the sound of hurried footsteps was followed by total silence. There was no more sleep for Maddalena that night. In the morning when Angelina and Clara came down from the attic, neither one mentioned the terror of the previous night.

The children, too, had learned the same unwritten law of the neighborhood. No one in the neighborhood ever spoke of the incident. It was as if it had never happened, but to Maddalena it added to the deep worries she felt for her daughters.

Maddalena also felt apprehension as she watched her young sons grow into manhood. The fact that Andy and Ricco would now learn a good trade alleviated some of her concerns since they would be busy working. Frankie was another matter. He disappeared each day with his friends, barely making it home for dinner. Though greatly relieved, she would ask, "Where have you been?"

"Oh, around," would be his casual answer as he plunged into his food.

Another fear plagued Maddalena. There was some suspicion that

Louie had a cousin connected to the Mafia, and she worried about Silia's safety when she spent time with Louie and this cousin.

Chapter Twenty-Seven

Felicetta and Assunta came with their children to visit the reunited family. It was especially heart-warming to share Maddalena's joy when she presented Angelina to them. Felicetta recalled the frightening time when she had to take the child home with her.

They were interrupted by the children racing into the house, excitedly calling out, "The *festa*, the *festa!*" The women walked out with them onto the front porch to see what was going on. Trucks were across the street, unloading materials to build the grandstand for the annual August celebration of the feast of the *'Madonna Del Pozzo'*. The grandstand fit perfectly into the narrow end of the empty lot, and would house the musicians who would provide music every night during the *festa*. At the wide end of the lot a merry-go-round would be set up and the hullabaloo created by the mixture of sound only added excitement to the occasion.

The three women sat on the front stoop and chatted until Maddalena suggested they go in for coffee to continue their conversation. Felicetta soon said her goodbyes since she had a long walk back to Hermitage Avenue and wanted to be home before dark. After she left, Assunta and her daughter Pietrina lingered a bit longer since they lived on the lower end of Kendall Street. Her friends felt Maddalena's joy and were grateful that, with Cristoforo at her side, the children growing up, and no new pregnancies, she finally had some respite from the unremitting pressures of her life. But still, always in the background, was the uncertainty of Massimo's fury.

As the weeks went by, it was difficult for Angelina to find her place in the family. She never went out in the street to play, but hung back on the stairs and watched. Silia, with her sweetness and kindness, went out of her way to make her sister comfortable.

"You know, Angelina," she offered, "you are going to enjoy the *festa*. It starts tomorrow, and you can watch the whole thing from the front steps."

Even the preparations for the *festa* were exciting. Almost every household bordering the empty lot created makeshift sidewalk stands where they either sold food or set up games. From his stand, Massimo sold the homemade sausage and pepper sandwiches that Maddalena and Silia made. Others offered roast beef sandwiches, barbequed lamb, fava beans in little paper cups, desserts, pastries and other Italian delicacies. Some sold cold drinks, wine, coffee, or the ever popular lemon ice scooped into a triangle of paper.

Other stands set up games of chance such as knocking down plastic milk bottles, throwing rings over bamboo canes, throwing pennies into a disk floating in a tub of water, and spinning a wheel while trying to pick the winning number. Prizes were mostly toys, the most coveted of which were the celluloid kewpie dolls with their nude bodies, little round bellies and a single tuft of hair in the middle of their heads.

When the bandstand was completed, strings of colored lights were stretched on the outline of the structure. The streets bordering the empty lot also had strings of lights from one lamppost to another. The night before the opening, the band rehearsed and the carousel was in place. Maddalena had somehow made an agreement with the man in charge of the carousel that he could use their family's bathroom in exchange for free rides for her children.

On opening night the neighborhood was in a frenzy. Houses were emptied as everyone moved onto the streets, stoops, stairs, and watched from railings. The older women gathered on the steps of Maddalena's house since it faced the bandstand directly. They sat, waited, and gossiped. Angelina sat on the top step close to the porch, waiting for her first *festa*, and Maddalena and Silia came out to take a quick break from sandwich making to see the opening. The stands were ready with the food and games.

At the long awaited starting time, the band began to play, the carousel whirled around and around, all the lights went on, and the people's excitement exploded in shouts everywhere. Suddenly they were in the midst of a fairyland instead of Chicago's worst slum neighborhood. People strolled from one stand to another, examining the possibilities. The band played Italian folk songs, opera, polkas and tarantellas. Some danced in the streets, which were blocked off to traffic. Teenagers sought out and eyed the opposite sex; old folks socialized and younger children scrambled wildly and freely in the safe, close community celebration. Shortly before midnight, with parents shooing their unwilling children to bed, the stands began to get cleaned up. When the hour struck and the music ended, instruments were put away, barricades removed, lights turned off, and the streets were emptied out. Yet, the promise of tomorrow hung over the neighborhood each night as the week-long celebration worked its way to the grand finale.

On the last day, the long awaited walk of the 'angel' took place on a wire stretched from the upper window of a building on one side of the street to a similar one on the opposite side. When the moment came and the angel took her first step onto the wire, a concerted gasp held the captive watchers breathless as she slowly inched her way to the other side of the street. When she moved from her last step on the wire safely to the windowsill, the held breaths exploded into a deafening community roar.

Although the eating, dancing and socializing took up the greater part of the week, the religious aspect dominated the afternoon of the last day. The statue of the Madonna was removed from San Callistus Church to a platform which was then carried through the streets on the shoulders of several men. As the procession moved down Kendall Street, a voice called out, "Who gives to the Madonna?" The paper money offered was pinned on the cape covering the statue and coins were tossed into a basket. When the statue had made its rounds, it was returned to the church. Then the fireworks display, eagerly anticipated all week long, would end the *festa* in a blaze of color, ear splitting noise and an acrid smell of smoking powder. Reluctantly, the people made their way home slowly. The clean-up would wait for the next day. In the morning, the bandstand and the carousel would be dismantled. The hearts of the people would wait for the next year's *festa*.

Chapter Twenty-Eight

Maddalena heard the news with a sinking heart. Cristoforo was moving to Arkansas. The Chicago winters caused him unbearable pain due to severe arthritis. Hearing that Hot Springs, Arkansas, offered natural relief in its hot mineral waters, he searched the newspapers for opportunities in that area. After visiting the springs and feeling relief from the pain, he decided to invest his savings in a one-hundred-and-sixty-acre plot of land near Little Rock. The land had a natural spring on it for water, and although it was too rocky to farm, he could raise sheep and goats.

"I must go," he sadly explained to Maddalena, "otherwise I will become a cripple and be no good to anyone."

They sat together in silence as they had so many times before. Maddalena could not help him in his dilemma, and he could no longer help buffer her against Massimo. No words could alleviate their pain of yet another separation and the fears they had for both of their futures. They had managed to come so far together.

After purchasing the land, Cristoforo settled into an old house that sat high upon a hill. With his horse and wagon, he drove the three miles to the tiny roadside stop that held a grocery store that included a post office. Turmbo, the store owner and postmaster, warned him, "Y'know, people around here don't take to strangers or foreigners."

Sure enough, when he came back from one of his trips, he found his house almost completely burned down. He understood that "*Stranieri* (strangers) are not welcome." He lived in what was left of the burned-out house and began to build a stone house on the lower level land that would eventually become the talk of the area. Pulling the stones out of the ground, he began piling stone upon stone. At the same time, he cleared one section to put in a garden and bought goats for milk and meat. Later he would send for Marie to join him, a woman he had met in a dental clinic in Chicago who was willing to become his housekeeper. He tried not to think of Maddalena and the children.

With Cristoforo gone, Maddalena lost not only loving support, but financial support as well, little as it had been. But she was grateful for his heartfelt gift of the wringer washing machine that would save her hours of drudgery and physical pain.

Once Cristoforo became established in his new home, Arkansas became a focal point in the family. Andy, having heard that Little Rock had a great baseball team and being unhappy with painting as a career, impulsively announced that he was going to hitchhike to visit Cristoforo and try his luck with Little Rock's baseball team. Panic struck Maddalena. Her son in unknown places, asking strangers for rides, riding on a freight train? He could be murdered! She begged him not to go, but the next day Andy disappeared without a word. For two days, she and Silia wondered where Andy might be, whether he was still alive, and if they would ever see him again. When the telegram came from Cristoforo that Andy had arrived safely, everyone breathed a sigh of relief.

Andy's trip inspired Ricco to follow. Even Angelina, at age sixteen, would go by bus with her friend Phyllis to spend the summer in Arkansas. Frankie, however, took a different turn. An invitation came for him to visit Anna Felice and Jim in California, where they had finally moved to escape the harsh winters. Settling in Huntington Park, a suburb of Los Angeles, they were in the process of starting an Italian restaurant. Their affection for Frankie had never diminished from the time of the horrible accident. Frankie was the tallest of Maddalena's three sons, with a widow's peak and thick black hair similar to his mother's. His glass eye caused people to give him a second look. Maddalena knew Frankie would be safer in California and maybe, at the same time, learn the restaurant business. It was with high hopes and a sigh of relief that she let him go.

Maddalena was thrilled that Cristoforo returned to Chicago for the summer to work because he couldn't earn enough money in Arkansas. He told her he would be back every summer. With that, and the children out of infancy, the part of her that ran freely in the piazza as a child, chasing the birds with a bit of mischief, was released and she could enjoy the pleasant things in her life. Her body let go of some of the chronic tension, and she smiled more often—although it was a smile always tinged with a sorrow reflected in her eyes. She struggled to learn how to use the wringer washing machine Cristoforo bought for her. It sat on the back porch storage area and she moved it into the kitchen for the clothes washing. It took awhile for her to get comfortable with it. Once, her fingers almost got caught in between the rollers of the wringer.

After dinner, rather than go down to the street, Maddalena sat on the front porch with Cristoforo, who tried to teach her English. At the same time she kept an eye on her three daughters playing on the sidewalk below.

As the end of August approached, she had to enroll Angelina in school. Clara was already going to the Catholic school, Saint Charles Borromeo, run by the Irish nuns and was accepted tuition free. Maddalena knew the nuns would agree to take Angelina also. As she and Cristoforo talked in the heat of the last August days, he agreed and both of them once again renewed their aspirations for a good education for the remaining three girls.

The boys were hardly ever home. Andy spent every moment after work on his baseball practice, and Ricco disappeared into the streets, as did Frankie. The two older boys had joined a 'Social Club' and had girl friends. Massimo was a shadow figure who came and went.

Before Cristoforo left to return home for the winter, Angelina brought a progress report home from school. He and Maddalena poured over it and smiled at each other.

"Look how well she's doing," Cristoforo commented.

"And—she likes going to school," Maddalena added.

They could hardly contain their excitement. All the failed efforts and the frustrations of the past were dissolved. Maybe the dream of educating the children could still come true. However, after a year of good progress, Maddalena was stunned when Angelina said the school wanted to talk to her.

Fearing the worst, Maddalena asked, "What did you do?"

Angelina answered, "Nothing."

Incredulous, seeing her dreams falling away, Maddalena persisted, "Why do they want to talk to me?"

Angelina answered tentatively, "I don't know."

A deep anxiety rose inside Maddalena, for the poor were afraid of all institutions ranging from hospitals, government relief with snoopy caseworkers, police, and even the schools. The powerlessness of the poor fueled the fears that often were confirmed by mistreatment or neglect.

She looked at her well-behaved daughter who seemingly loved school and couldn't imagine what she might have done to cause this disaster. The next day, with Angelina in hand, filled with apprehension, Maddalena appeared at the entrance of the school and was directed to a special room apart from the classrooms. There a nun sat in a small space with a tiny desk, a piano and two chairs. She pointed to the chairs for Maddalena and Angelina to be seated while she sat on the piano bench. She spoke in a soft gentle voice, "I'm Sister Mary Odelia. I teach piano here at Saint Charles. I'm sorry but I have to let you know that it has been several weeks and you haven't paid for Angelina's lessons."

Maddalena barely whispered the question, "Lessons?"

"Yes," answered the nun. "She has been taking piano lessons and they cost twenty-five cents a lesson."

Maddalena was mute. She thought, "Twenty-five cents a lesson?" How often she had told God if she could only have fifty cents a week regularly, she could do so much for her children. Now she was being told—twenty-five cents a week for a lesson? For what? A piano lesson? She could not put it together.

The nun spoke again, explaining, "You know—six weeks of piano lessons cost one dollar and fifty cents."

By now Angelina was terrified. She was sure her mother would banish her back to Zi' Anna Felice. She remembered the day this very same nun had come into the classroom and asked if anyone in the class would like to take piano lessons. She had eagerly raised her hand, but no mention had been made of money. Now she was devastated that she had created this big problem for her mother.

Maddalena looked at her frightened daughter. Whether or not she understood how this situation had come about, she would not betray her child. She hung her head and mumbled in her broken English, "I'm sorry. We have no money. My husband doesn't work. We are on relief."

The dreaded moment for Angelina had arrived. Not only might she be banished, but she loved her lessons and now she saw her dream about to vanish.

Sister Mary Odelia liked Angelina and felt she had talent. Rather than drop her as a student, she would find a way. Finally, she said, "Well, she is a good student. She can work for her lessons. Don't worry about the money any more. Thank you for coming, Mrs. Chiuppi."

They walked home in silence, each in their own world of thought. Maddalena tried to fathom spending twenty-five cents a week for a lesson on how to play the piano; Angelina, jubilant that her mother was not angry, was relieved that her cherished lessons would continue. From that day forth, Angelina went to school early, stayed during the lunch hour, and after classes, did whatever was asked of her, while finding a refuge from the noisy chaos at home.

Chapter Twenty-Nine

A new wave of excitement stirred up the neighborhood. The news had spread everywhere. "They got Dillinger." In disbelief, the people young and old asked, "How? Where?"

"Yeah, the cops killed him. They'll be bringing his body in pretty quick," was the follow-up answer.

Dillinger's exploits, as a bank robber who defied getting caught, were a constant topic in the neighborhood. When he was finally caught, betrayed by a girlfriend at a local movie house, the adults rejoiced but the children saw him as an anti-hero and were disappointed.

"Let's go to the morgue and see him!" the children shouted.

The children gathered in small groups and walked the few blocks to the county morgue, which would be Dillinger's final destination. The groups stood silently outside the building, trying to catch the officials bringing in his corpse. Angelina and Clara were among them.

Every so often an arrival brought a corpse to the morgue gate, and the bravest of the group called out, "Is that Dillinger?" The usual answer was, "Get lost, kid." Angelina, standing with the crowd, felt a chill every time a covered body was lifted out of the police wagon and onto the gurney that would eventually slide the remains onto the cold slabs in the walls. Again, a voice rang out; "Is that Dillinger?" and the answer came back, "Drop dead, punk!" The excitement began to wane when the groups realized that nothing was going to be revealed. He might have been brought in and they wouldn't have even known it. The crowd slowly broke up and everyone started for home, feeling they had lost their big chance—not knowing really for what. A little shudder went through Angelina when she thought that a famous gangster was right here in their neighborhood. It didn't matter that he was dead—it was <u>his</u> body.

This same year Angelina was to graduate from elementary school. The nuns were so pleased with her industrious and serious application to everything set before her, whether it was her job duties or her studies or the piano lessons, that they arranged for her to receive a work scholarship to the prestigious girls' Catholic high school located across the street from the grammar school. It was a private school, run by the same order of nuns, and offered a strict, academic program geared to college preparation. Saint Mary's High School was known throughout the city and served mostly girls from the outlying suburbs who came by bus or by car to the inner city school. Rarely were the neighborhood girls able to attend.

When Angelina received the scholarship, Maddalena and Silia were delighted and presented her with flowers. Again, Maddalena wished Cristoforo could be there. It would mean so much to him. When he arrived to work that summer, he beamed a big smile to Angelina and his pride showed, giving the encouragement she did not get from her father who, as usual, was not interested.

She worked that summer at the high school convent, and when she entered school in the fall, she was informed that she also would study piano and play the cello in the orchestra. Later, learning to play brass instruments was added to her piano lessons, and eventually the nuns had Angelina lead the band as the drum majorette. She took all this in stride and set herself to succeed at everything. Even when she realized that it took her four hours every night to do her homework, she was not deterred. At times, Clara complained that her sister never had to help in the kitchen. Maddalena gently would say, "Let her be. She has more than enough to do."

Clara looked at Angelina. Her sister was either playing the piano or studying or reading a book, and because of that, she got away with not doing any work around the house. At times, Clara resented her. At times, she admired her. Sometimes she compared herself to Angelina in that Angelina had very curly hair and Clara's hair was straight. Clara was teased often enough that the milk man must have brought her into a family of curly-haired people. Yet, they had the same hazel eyes. But mostly, Clara couldn't sit still as long as Angelina could. She needed to be outside where she could move and run and be with her friends. Clara was playful, mischievous, vivacious and energetic.

The one indoor activity Clara enjoyed was helping Maddalena cook. The almost daily meal of *pasta e fazool* (pasta and beans) was boring. It was the special days when Maddalena made *gnocchi, ravioli,* or *polenta* that Clara liked getting her hands into the dough. Rolling out the *gnocchi* dough into long narrow strips across the kitchen table and then cutting it into one-inch pieces were the first two steps to start the process. While the water was set to boil, and the "red gravy" (the name used for tomato sauce) simmered on the stove, Clara and Maddalena cut the strips into one-inch pieces. Using two fingers they then flipped each piece so that it folded within itself. The gnocchi were then ready to be tossed into the boiling water. When the *gnocchi* was served with the savory gravy, the children were ecstatic.

The *ravioli,* however, took more time and after Maddalena stretched the homemade dough on a sheet on the bed to be ready for the filling, Clara, Caroline, and often Angelina, would gather around the table to cut the dough into each square, taking turns placing the spinach and creamy ricotta cheese in the center of the square, then folding the dough over the filling. Finally, Angelina would crimp the edges of the square with the tines of a fork while Caroline stuck a needle in the top of each square to release the air. Now each square was eased into the boiling water, removed carefully, sauced, sprinkled with cheese and then served to the children who relished them with great pleasure.

On *polenta* day, Maddalena stirred the cornmeal carefully because it would burn very easily. When it was ready, the steaming cornmeal was spread out directly onto a large hardwood board that was set on top of the kitchen table. The yellow mushy cornmeal was about an inch high and swathed over with the gravy and a final sprinkling of white, freshly grated cheese. The girls gathered around the board. Each person outlined her share with her fork and *polenta* was eaten directly off the board. It slid easily into the mouth, and the mixture created a heavenly flavor that encouraged holding it in the mouth and rolling it around to fully savor it before swallowing it. The outlined share was never enough, and everyone waited hungrily to pounce on any leftovers. When the meal was over, the board was scraped clean. The delicious aromas lingered in the air as the board was stored away for the next *polenta* feast.

Maddalena paid most of her attention to the "gravy." When she could, she would get pork neck bones and simmer them all day in the gravy until the meat fell away from the bones. The second day, it simmered with a cheap cut of chuck beef and finally the third day, for the Sunday meal, she added meatballs. This was the basis for the flavor of the gravy and the staple for most meals, including the traditional dinners on Thursday and Sunday. For Maddalena, cooking for and feeding her family was a joy. "*Mangia, Mangia,*" she would urge them.

Finding the money to buy even the cheapest cuts of meat or groceries was a battle for the city's poor. There was no space around tenement apartments to put in gardens. Credit at the grocery store or the meat market was a last resort. When Massimo was at his worst, he informed the storekeeper not to give Maddalena any more credit.

One day, Angelina rushed into the house and called out, "Ma, Ma, I have a job!" Maddalena was in the kitchen and as Angelina came into the room, they sat down and faced each other over the kitchen table.

In a panic, Maddalena asked, "You haven't left school, have you?"

"Oh no, Ma. I would never do that. This job is only two hours a week."

"Where is it? What will you be doing? Is it a safe place?" Maddalena fearfully questioned her.

"It's okay, Ma. My piano teacher got a call that they needed someone to play the piano for dancing classes at this Boys' Club. I'll get twenty-five cents an hour. That means I'll get fifty cents a week I can give you."

"Fifty cents a week!" exclaimed Maddalena. "Fifty cents a week?" she repeated, more emphatically. "Just to play the piano?" she added, incredulously.

"Yeah, Ma, Sister said they are good people. They have this place where kids can go after school to play in the gym, or take classes. It's called 'Off the Street Club'. It's over on Van Buren and Ashland—I can walk. I start next Friday from seven to nine at night."

"That's out of our neighborhood. I don't like you walking home that late at night alone. Can Clara go with you?"

"I think so. Kids of all ages go there, you know. I think Clara will like it. They teach dancing and a bunch of other stuff. You know how she likes to dance."

"Are you sure they pay twenty five cents an hour?" she again asked in a non-believing tone.

Angelina smiled, "Yeah, Ma. That's what Sister said."

The next Friday, with Clara in tow, Angelina played for her first dance class in which Clara participated. Clara loved it. When they got home, Angelina, filled with pride, handed her mother the fifty cents. Maddalena, filled with gratitude, said, "Tomorrow you will go and buy day-old bread for us to eat."

Chapter Thirty

Though the children went to the Catholic school, the church played little part in Maddalena's life. Her visible moments of acknowledging God came at outbursts in moments of desperation, when her efforts to feed or clothe her children were in jeopardy, or when Massimo's violence escalated beyond control. Raising her face to the ceiling, she would lift her hands, shaking them. She would cry out in frustration, "*Gesu Cristo*, what did I do to deserve this? Did I pull your beard or something that you treat me so badly?" After lamenting her fate, she resignedly would go back to her work.

No priest ever showed an interest in the family. The only outsiders who consistently showed up were the caseworker, checking on the status of government support—searching for hidden signs of prosperity— and the gas man, who came to read the meter on a haphazard sort of schedule. Maddalena, in an attempt to save every penny, had learned how to turn off the gas meter. Then gauging when the gas man should reappear, the children were posted to watch for him. When he was spotted, they rushed home calling out, "Ma! Ma! The gas man!" Hurriedly and fearfully, Maddalena would run to turn the meter back on just in time.

Although doctors made home visits for those who could pay, none ever showed up at Maddalena's house. It was Zi' Filomena she turned to in times of illness, a woman well known in the neighborhood for her healing powers and other mysterious abilities. Her slight, bent figure, dressed in black with a thick black shawl draped over her head, was quickly recognizable. She walked with her arms gathered together as if she were holding within herself all the unknown solutions to both psychological and physical human pain. She emanated an aura of mystery. Respected by the elders for her magic powers, feared by the children for these same powers, she was often called upon to minister healing to the sick.

After one of the *festas*, Angelina developed a headache and stiff neck so severe she could not turn her head. "Clara," Maddalena called out from the front porch. "Go fetch Zi' Filomena. Tell her Angelina is sick."

Clara put down the pinners ball she was about to aim at the red bricks on the building next door. "Aw, Ma," she called back, in a pleading voice, "I don't want to go to her house. She's a witch—she puts spells on people."

When Maddalena insisted, Clara went off, dragging her feet as she walked the two blocks up Kendall Street and down Almond Street with her fingers crossed, and praying for God's protection. Before she reached the dreaded house on the corner, she crossed the street from it, looked at it as she crossed herself several times, took a deep breath and quickly ran over and knocked on the door. This was a brave move since hardly any child would walk on the same side of the street where the house was located, much less walk directly to the door. The possibility of being drawn in by Zi' Filomena's magic power was chilling.

Clara shook with fear as she waited. When the door opened, she tried not to look at Zi' Filomena and gasped, "My mother needs you." Then she turned and vanished like a wraith into the distance.

As Zi' Filomena left her house to go to Maddalena's, heads turned, faces peered from windows, and children scattered to make way as she headed out on her healing mission. Once she arrived, Maddalena pointed to the suffering figure on the couch, and Zi' Filomena began to issue orders for the required setting. All shades must be drawn, everyone was to leave the house except Maddalena, and no one was allowed to enter until she had completed the healing process. Once these orders were satisfied, she called for a dish of warm oil, kneeled at Angelina's side in the quiet, darkened room and softly spoke her unintelligible incantations. Along with the mumbled sounds, she dipped her fingers into the warm oil and began to make crosses on Angelina's forehead and the back of her neck. Maddalena, standing quietly in the background, could see Angelina relaxing. After completing the healing, Zi' Filomena, blotted off the excess oil with a soft towel, and gave her final instructions to keep the child quiet and warm for an hour and to avoid the malocchio (the evil eye) in the future. As she left, Maddalena gratefully pressed her hand and said, "*Grazie.*" With a slight nod, Zi' Filomena was gone. Noting that Angelina was dozing, Maddalena went out to warn the children not to come in until she called them.

Maddalena shuddered at Zi' Filomena's comment about the evil eye—the *malocchio*. Had she not protected her daughter from the prolonged, intensive gaze that certain people could cast on an individual, thus creating illness and bad luck? She would be more careful to put a pinch of salt in Angelina's pocket or to pin a piece of red ribbon on her sleeve, and to remind her to hide her hand and tuck her thumb under her fingers if someone seemed to look at her too long. She also worried that she had seen some people with tiny doll figures stuck with pins intending to cause illness or even death to an unsuspecting enemy. Maddalena agonized over the fear of the unknown.

Chapter Thirty-One

With Cristoforo gone, Massimo escalated his grumblings into a full scale roar of cursing and yelling. The weekends were the worst. He and his cronies would spend all of their time in the back room of Vendu's corner candy store gambling and drinking. Sometimes they would sing songs from the old country, vying with each other for more creative versions with longer and longer made-up verses, bellowing at the top of their lungs. As the evening wore on and the wine flowed, the songs would change to screaming curses. The group would scrape their chairs away from the table to better wave their arms at each other in a threatening fashion. Vendu would hurry to the back room when that happened and call out, "*Ma, scusi?...* do you want the police to come around?"

As they quieted down, the games started to break up and they soon staggered toward their homes. Carrying with him a full load of his anger and his hatred for Maddalena, Massimo stomped into the house and woke up the children, who froze with fright. Maddalena waited for the worst. How she wished she had followed through on her plan years ago to go downtown to the judge and turn herself and her children in for a different home away from the constant fear, anxiety, and chaos. How she wished she had not let Assunta talk her out of it.

Massimo roared into their room and ordered her to get herself up and fix him a sandwich and coffee, yelling, "You're the reason for all-a my trouble, and, some-a day-a, a-ma gonna kill-a you!"

The threats were in Italian or broken English, since he had barely learned the language of his adopted country. The children, however, caught between the two worlds, spoke English and could understand part of the Italian. Their father's threat they had heard over and over like the litanies of the church—they fully understood and trembled. After he ate his sandwich and drank his coffee, muttering the whole time, he again ordered Maddalena to leave the dishes and go to bed with him.

By the time he fell asleep, Maddalena, weeping silently, quietly crawled out of bed and went to comfort the children. The next morning, Massimo would disappear until late in the evening.

Angelina was the oldest of the three girls. His words rang in her ears, "Some-a day-a, a-ma gonna kill-a you!" She wondered in what way he would do it, and how they would survive without their mother.

"Why does my father hate my mother?" she asked herself. There was no one to turn to for an answer. She became Maddalena's 'look-out', often sitting in the gangway outside the window of the basement bedroom where he slept off his drunken bouts, listening for his awakening sounds so she could quickly warn her mother. While she sat patiently waiting, her thoughts drifted over the life they led. She didn't understand any of it, but she knew this was not what she wanted. She did not want to depend upon a man who would abuse her day after day, like her father. She would go to school, learn to support herself and not have to depend on anyone else. This decision would dominate her life.

Several children were chasing each other down the street when Clara broke away and hurtled into the gangway—almost colliding with Angelina.

"Sh! Sh!" Angelina whispered and grabbed her. "Pa's asleep and we don't want to wake him up."

The two sisters looked at each other—the one quiet and contained, the other boisterous and outgoing. Angelina worried about her sister, who sometimes used words like 'damn' and 'hell', who never combed her hair, and who raced like an electric current throughout the house and the neighborhood streets. Clara viewed her sister as a stranger whose ways she didn't understand.

Brushing past her sister, Clara dashed down the long gangway to the back yard where another long flight of stairs led onto the back porch, then into the kitchen.

Angelina, hearing stirrings from Massimo, ran down the gangway following Clara, and as she entered the kitchen, called out, "Ma! Ma! He's awake!"

This was the signal for alertness, for one could never tell if he would be moody or explosive. One time Maddalena had put a tablecloth on the kitchen table to celebrate the birthday of Mary, Silia's daughter. In the midst of a rage, Massimo yanked the cloth off the table, screaming angry curses and sending cups, plates, and the birthday cake flying in every direction. His rage, whether expressed or held in abeyance, was an ever present threat.

The times he chased her around the house sent the children calling to the neighbors for help. There was no phone. And neighbors were not inclined to get involved. It was common to hear screaming fights in many of the households. Maddalena often fled into the street, calling to the children to follow her as she sought refuge at Assunta's house.

One always waited in fear for the next episode. When word came that Cristoforo was coming back to work for the summer, everyone breathed a sigh of relief.

Chapter Thirty-Two

Angelina closed her eyes and played her pieces on the kitchen table, her imaginary piano. The real piano was at school. She had found her solace—she could make music. Every morning she left the house early to get to the practice rooms provided for the students. At lunch and after school she worked for her lessons, grateful not to have to go home until she absolutely had to.

The house was not totally devoid of music, for Louie, Silia's husband, played the drums in a band. Late at night, the band came to the house and serenaded Silia with lilting Italian waltzes and perky tarantellas. The music wafted into the bedrooms of the children, some of whom listened for a moment, then went back to sleep. Maddalena, however, put on the spaghetti water and fried up some sausages and peppers. As she spooned the gravy and sausage mixture over the spaghetti, the men yelled to each other with raucous laughter in a lascivious, supplicating imitation of a female voice, "*Salciccia*, oh master." The innuendo relating the sausage to a male organ was not lost on the innocent ears present. Still, the music of the serenade was not lost either. Angelina was entranced and stayed awake to hear the very last note played and inadvertently, the coarse remarks.

The lack of a piano in the house was not lost on Louie either. On a crisp October day, he announced that he had found a piano for seven dollars and that it would be delivered the next day. When it appeared at the front door and the delivery men were bringing it into the living room,

Angelina ran up to the top of the steps leading to the attic and crouched below the trap door. She watched breathlessly as they placed the piano against the living room wall. Once the men left, everyone called up to her, "Eh! What are you doing, *stupida?* Come down and play for us."

Maddalena, whose joy knew no bounds, pleaded with her, but to no avail. Angelina was rooted to the spot, unable to move, holding her breath. The piano was a living, breathing object. It could make music. To have it there, in her home, to play anytime she wanted was more than she could bear.

Maddalena said, "Leave her alone. She'll come down when she's ready."

So they gave up on her and went back to what they had been doing. When the living room was empty, Angelina moved very slowly, working her way down the stairs, and sat on the bench, placing unmoving fingers lovingly over the silent keys. Her cup was too full—she had to let it run over until she was ready to drink. Maddalena silently watched from out of sight in the kitchen. "Oh, Cristoforo," her heart called out, "if only you could be here to see this. Your joy like mine would soar to heaven."

Silia had watched the piano being delivered but had to get back to her children, who were napping. They had moved to a second-story flat in the apartment building next door. Silia returned later with her daughters, expecting Angelina to play the piano for them. But Angelina, still too overwhelmed, had returned upstairs.

"What's wrong with Angelina?" Silia asked Maddalena, who only shook her head and shrugged.

"It's too much for her. When she's ready, she'll play," Maddalena cautioned Silia.

Later, while they worked in the kitchen, they heard the music start. At this point, Massimo came in. He gave a casual glance at the girl playing a piano he had never seen and moved quickly to the kitchen for his food.

It was a brisk, cool October morning. The glow of Indian Summer had faded, the days were getting shorter, and the women drew their shawls a little tighter as they left their perches on the sidewalk to go back into the house for the night.

The Great Depression was in full swing. A pall lay over the neighborhood. Most of the men had lost their jobs and the young men loitered on the street unable to find work. The women asked each other, "How are we going to feed our children? What will we do when the winter sets in? How will we heat our houses?"

The onset of winter terrified them. When they came up with no answers, they shook their heads helplessly. Many of them were already on relief, getting the basic beans, pasta and flour from the government. Others would have to apply for help and face the possibility of rejection. There was nowhere to turn. Desperation changed the October coolness into a chill that seeped into the marrow of their bones like the ever-present, penetrating Chicago wind.

Maddalena sat alone in the kitchen, having gotten the children off to school. Massimo was gone to whatever he did, with no comment. Maddalena stared at the official looking envelope that had just arrived in the mail. A stab of fear pierced her insides as she slowly opened the fold and pulled out the contents. The words were illegible to her, but she sensed their formality. She wished Cristoforo were there to read it to her. She would have to wait until Angelina came home from school.

Filled with foreboding, she paced, wandering from the kitchen through the dining room and into the living room, where she glanced out of the windows at the empty lot and the street below. Turning around she retraced her steps through the dining room and back into the kitchen. Unable to settle her mind, she decided to go to Assunta's house. Although she knew that Assunta also could not read, at least she felt that they could look at the letter together and try to figure it out. Grabbing a sweater, she started down the flight of stairs leading to the street and turned toward Assunta's house. She was so preoccupied with her thoughts that she didn't even realize she had bumped into Assunta in front of Vendu's candy store on the corner.

"Maddalena," called out Assunta, "where are you going in such a hurry? I was just coming to your house to see you."

Startled, Maddalena pulled back and stared at Assunta as if it were hard to give up the thoughts that had taken over her mind. "Oh, okay," she stammered, "I was just coming to your house to show you this letter." Maddalena blurted out, the words tumbling over each other, "I thought you could help me figure it out."

"What letter?" Assunta asked.

Maddalena waved it in the air and said, "Let's go to my house and have some coffee and I'll show it to you."

As the aroma of the coffee filled the kitchen, they perused the letter intently as if it would divulge its contents by the force of their wills. They looked at each other and realized there was no hope of figuring it out. All they could agree on was that it was definitely something official.

As Maddalena rose to refill their coffee cups, they heard the front door burst open and the voices of the three girls returning from school calling out, "We're home, Ma, we're home!"

Settling the coffee pot back on the stove, Maddalena greeted the girls and pulled Angelina aside, saying, "We need you to read this letter."

She handed the letter to Angelina and waited. The two women exchanged worried glances. It seemed to take forever for Angelina to silently read the letter. When she finally looked up at them, they saw that her face had turned pale.

"What? What?" they prodded frantically.

Looking at her mother, Angelina read in a strained voice, "This is an eviction notice. You have sixty days to move out of this property."

Unable to take in the information, the two women sat shaken and speechless . . . "move out of this property" . . . the words could not penetrate Maddalena's brain . . . "this property, this property . . . move out . . . move out."

'This property' was her home. The words seemed unreal but her home was real. Barely able to get the words to cross her lips, she mumbled, "What? Move out of our house? Where would we go?"

Angelina went on, "They say you haven't paid the mortgage."

Maddalena responded, choking on her dry throat and weak breath, "We barely have enough money to get food and coal for the winter."

Assunta tried to calm Maddalena down, saying, "It must be some mistake. Don't be upset, Maddalena."

Turning to Angelina, Assunta suggested, "Read it all over again and very slowly."

They hovered over her, waiting with bated breath to see if there would be a change in her face. Angelina finally looked up at them, nodding her head, and saying, "It's just as I told you. This letter is from the bank saying that we have to move out in 60 days for not paying the mortgage." With a voice cracking with fear, she added, "Where will we go, Ma?"

Visions rolled around in Maddalena's mind of all their meager furniture sitting out on the sidewalk. Massimo would make sure to store his wine barrels with one of his card-playing friends. The rest would be up to her.

She couldn't imagine where she and the children would go. Silia had moved to a tiny apartment in the Cabrini-Green housing project. Assunta and Felicetta would want to help but they too could not accommodate the large family.

"I don't know," Maddalena answered, the words squeaking out from her dry throat.

A brutal dark cloud of anxiety settled over her, triggering her mind backward to her former disasters such as the early illnesses of the children. She remembered Andrew's diphtheria and subsequent chronic lung problems, Enrico's severe burns, Frankie's convulsions, and the death of baby Angelo. Then there was the time Andrew left home to hitchhike to Arkansas, and the continuous fear from Massimo's unpredictable fury. All the experiences she had endured flooded her brain. She felt it would explode at any moment.

Angelina looked at her mother's face. A widow's peak framed the thick black hair now sprinkled with gray. Her eyes, reflecting a deep sadness and sometimes a twinkle of humor, now looked empty and far away. Angelina's love for her mother overcame her. She wanted to cry out, to somehow fix everything, to make it all right, to protect her mother, but she felt powerless. And then she thought of the one source they had always turned to in the past—Cristoforo.

"Ma, couldn't Zio Cristoforo help us?" she asked.

A shadow crossed Maddalena's face. She missed her brother deeply since he had moved to Arkansas. "No," she answered, "he's trying to build a house. No, we can't even tell him about this. It would break his heart that he cannot help."

A silence fell over them, each lost in their own thoughts. Angelina recalled the years she had spent with her aunt, Anna Felice in Oakfield, New York—the quiet, orderly life, based on running the restaurant, the boarding house, and the family home. Order and discipline were exerted by Anna Felice on everyone, marked by occasional skirmishes with Jim and outright screaming battles with her younger brother Giulio. One night, after a major blow-up, Anna Felice ended up chasing after him with a frying pan in her hand. Soon after, he was asked to leave. And yet, in general, it was a peaceful existence with a quiet day-to-day predictability.

Angelina's thoughts moved forward to her long-awaited return to her mother. She remembered being totally unprepared for the chaos and darkness in the home and her father's heavy-handed treatment of her mother. Yet the happiness she found in being with her mother overshadowed everything. Now, her mother faced this new dilemma that seemed to have no solution.

Assunta broke the silence, saying, "I need to go home now. I will talk to Felicetta to see what we can do."

As she prepared to leave, Maddalena, trying to hold on to her loving and supportive presence, said, "I'll walk you part way." They left, leaving Angelina musing until the voices of her sisters, Clara and Caroline, called her to the streets.

There were no books, newspapers, magazines, radio or telephone in the house, only old newspapers or discarded phone books or catalogs to be used in place of toilet paper. What went on in the outside world seeped in from the talk that got around in the streets. As the days went by, the name 'Roosevelt' began to emerge. Maddalena inquired, "Who is this 'Roosevelt'?" When she found out that he was the President of the United States, it meant nothing to her. "What difference does it make?" she thought.

In a few weeks the neighborhood began to change. Suddenly the jobless young men began disappearing from the streets, and Ricco was talking about joining a group called the CCC's (the Civilian Conservation Corps). Maddalena's fear of the unknown came up until Ricco explained that it meant he had a temporary job with the government. He would work in the forests of upper Michigan, planting trees and clearing out the land. He would receive three meals a day, have a place to sleep, and earn twenty-five dollars a month. This program was set up by this 'Roosevelt', whose name was becoming more and more of a household word.

Maddalena was elated. And yet, happy as she was that Ricco would be in a good place, the specter of eviction invaded her thoughts.

The big news eventually surfaced. Roosevelt took over the failed banks, formed a government-run Home Owner's Loan Corporation, and in so doing, he also took over the banks' mortgages. This news was capped by the information that caused Maddalena and all the other women to be jubilant. Any family on relief would have their mortgages paid for by the government. No one would be evicted.

When she fully realized this, Maddalena dropped to her knees, raised her eyes to the heavens and proclaimed, "*Gesu Cristo, mille grazie e anche a te signor Roosevelt!*" (Jesus Christ, a million thanks, and also to you, Mister Roosevelt!)

Chapter Thirty-Three

Within the next three years, Maddalena saw all three of her boys get married. Andy and Ricco settled back into painting with their brother-in-law, Louie, and would eventually go into the business for a major part of their lives. Andy and Ricco began courting two girls they met at the neighborhood social club whom they ended up marrying. Andy married Angeline Iovino, and Ricco married Annie Durante. The two weddings were celebrated in true Italian style. First, the services in Saint Charles Church drew friends and neighbors. As the newly married couple emerged from the church, sugar-coated almonds (*confetti*) were tossed at them, and the children dashed in every direction, grabbing all they could until not one remained on the ground.

A large hall was rented, a live band hired to play Italian style dance music, and the usual roast beef sandwiches were prepared. The walls of the hall were lined with chairs from which the older women gazed at the scene and passed remarks to each other concerning the dress of the young people, the state of the pregnancies that were visible, the babies, and the behavior of other people's children. Fresh peanuts were abundant with shells discarded everywhere. The wedding party sat in glorious style at a special table. Wine flowed, the adults had coffee, and the children drank pop.

At the height of the evening, everyone was poised for the Grand March. At the proper moment, the bride and groom left their table and placed themselves in the center of the room. The wedding party lined up behind them in couples followed by the parents, relatives, and friends. At the end of the line the children pranced to form the tail end of the march. When the music began, the procession began. Around and around the hall they circled until the music came to a halt. At that point, all the couples except the wedding party fell away. A circle was formed by the wedding party, and into the empty space the bridal couple began the first dance with the others gradually joining them until the dance floor was filled. The children also got onto the floor and did their creative, wild gyrations. It was an open-ended celebration. By the end of the evening, the exhausted bride and groom stole away, parents rounded up resisting children who had left their legacy of peanut shells behind them, and the older women moved slowly to go home. The wedding included everyone in the family; a wedding was a family affair. No one was left at home.

Frankie, on the other hand, did not have a traditional wedding with the usual festivities. He and Elsie Florio had a quiet wedding with only the two families present. They moved in with Maddalena, for Frankie went back and forth to California to work with Anna Felice.

Now with Silia and all the boys married, the Sunday noonday meal of spaghetti and meatballs had an expanded set of mouths to feed. The house vibrated with the comings and goings of the older children, the younger children and the new babies. Andy had three children close together: Robert, Louise, and Madelyn. Ricco brought his two little ones, Annie and Henry Carl. All this thrilled Maddalena. She was happiest when surrounded by her children and now her grandchildren. She smiled more often.

In addition to this happiness, Cristoforo was returning for his summer work. With Marie caring for the animals back in Arkansas, he was free to earn the money they needed for their winter supplies. There was always work to be had in Chicago.

After he arrived, they sat down together to catch up on the goings-on of their separate lives. When Maddalena broke the disturbing news about Silia to Cristoforo, he was so taken aback he could hardly respond.

"Yes." Maddalena repeated. "Silia wants to divorce her husband. I've tried and tried to talk her out of it, but she says she is unhappy because he is mean to her. I just don't know what to do."

Cristoforo drew back his head in disbelief.

"Wasn't he the one who bought Angelina the piano?" he asked.

"Yes," she quickly answered.

"And wasn't he the one who bought the first Christmas tree for the children?" he continued.

She didn't answer immediately, her thoughts going back to the excitement of the children that morning when Louie had brought the live tree into the house. The strings of lights had transformed the house into a fairyland. The children were awed by it.

"Ma! Ma! Look!" they had shouted in excitement.

For days Caroline had sat quietly and stared at it while Clara had danced around it, fingering the crisp green needles and sniffing the fresh pine smell.

Finally, Maddalena brought her thoughts back to her brother's question and answered, "Yes, you're right."

"Well then?" Cristoforo asked. "What could be so bad that she would want a divorce?"

"I can only tell you she says he is mean to her and it has been going on for a long time. I don't know for sure, but I think he hits her," Maddalena responded.

Cristoforo frowned. "Maddalena, this is America. Silia is a good girl, and we have no right to tie her down. It's been over ten years, and if things are still not better for her, let her decide."

A sense of relief came over her. She did not want her daughter to be trapped in the same situation that she herself was in—a forced marriage followed by a miserable life. Yet Maddalena dreaded the storm of criticism that would be unleashed. There would be much gossip and talk about *"la disgrazia"* among the neighbors. Divorce was a shameful act—against the church and against the family. Italian women did not divorce their husbands.

"Let them talk," Cristoforo offered.

Maddalena agreed. Her children were more important than the neighbors' approval. She was not close to any of them anyway, except for Assunta. Assunta and Felicetta would want the best for Silia.

She refilled his cup of coffee and asked, "What is it like where you live?"

Cristoforo drew his chair closer to hers and gave a deep sigh. "Ah, *bellissimo!* (beautiful), more like our mountain home in Italy. I live in the Ozark mountains with many trees; with a quiet that is only disturbed by the gentle rustle of leaves in the trees when the wind blows through, with fresh clean air, and the water—ah—the water. We have to walk a long way to get it, but it comes from a deep underground spring and tastes like the nectar of the gods. Even the mountain water of our village cannot compare. Everything is green—the sunsets are spectacular. I wish you could come there to live. It would be so much better for the children."

She sighed and tried to visualize such a place. The dirt and noise and anxieties of the big city made her want to scoop up the children and follow him. Instead, she said, "I'm so happy for you."

"Now I have almost finished my house," Cristoforo continued, "they can never turn me out."

At that moment a great commotion broke out in the street. The noise was ear-splitting. They ran to the front windows and saw that the coal truck had dumped the winter supply of coal on the sidewalk. Cristoforo always waited to return to Arkansas until after the coal delivery. He helped carry it to the storage shed underneath the stairs leading to the upper story of the house. The coal man was the harbinger of winter, the reminder of the precious last days of autumn.

Winter was always a threat. Maddalena dreaded it. How to keep her children from getting sick in a very cold, drafty house and with few warm clothes was a constant challenge. One year Angelina froze her big toe from the lack of good shoes. Maddalena always rose very early to start a fire in the potbellied stove to heat up the house before the children got up. It was lovely to wake in the morning, look out the window and see the world clothed in the soft white beautiful garment of the first snow, but it was another thing to send her children out into it unprotected. Unexpected illness was greater in winter, and this reality hung over her head.

If one survived the winter, a new fear would arise at the onset of spring. A gradual influx of gypsies began to take over the empty stores, covering the windows with Bon Ami cleanser so no one could see inside. There they squatted, venturing forth to beg, steal, or tell fortunes. The women wore several long, brightly covered voluminous skirts, one overlaid on top of the other. Their necks and arms were covered with an assortment of necklaces and bracelets, and always on their ears hung huge loops of gold.

Every year the call went out throughout the neighborhood—"The gypsies are here." Mothers warned their children never to walk in front of Bon Ami'd windows or they might be snatched inside, never to be seen again, or that a gypsy could grab a small child off the street, cover him or her with her voluminous skirt, and again the child would be stolen, never to be seen again. No one knew where the gypsies came from or where they went when they left. By summer they were gone. The mothers counted their children, who, fascinated with the gypsies, had walked as close as they could to the Bon Ami'd windows, yet kept a healthy distance when a gypsy walked down their street. The lure of the gypsies and the excitement it generated for the children finally was over. Calm was restored to the neighborhood, and a sense of relief comforted the mothers.

Chapter Thirty-Four

Maddalena was appalled to find that she was pregnant once again. She was forty-two and had been enjoying the release from the constant care of numerous infants. It felt daunting to her, but there was nothing she could do. It was still a struggle to feed and clothe her children. Massimo brought in no money, and if by chance he earned some, he kept it for himself for his 'dago ropes', the De Nobili cigars, and the grapes he would need to make his supply of wine. He had just completed the year's wine-making and had three casks in the wine cellar to serve him the next year.

It was the end of September, and Massimo was feeling quite satisfied with himself. This particular evening, Maddalena was sitting on the fourth step up from the sidewalk, trying to stay cool, large in her almost seventh month of pregnancy. Keeping her mother company, Angelina sat on the upper iron rail with her feet hooked into the lower rail. Massimo appeared, eating a chocolate bar. He walked back and forth past Maddalena, a smirk on his face as he chewed the delicious candy. From time to time, he intentionally farted as he went by her and continued his promenade until he finished the chocolate bar. Then he took off for Vendu's to spend his evening playing cards with his friends. The incident would leave a mark on Angelina. Her heart ached for her mother and she again asked herself the unanswerable question, "Why does my father hate my mother?"

The following January, Maddalena delivered her ninth and final child and named him Michael. Angelina listened as the midwife and friends worked through the night in the bedroom next to hers. The next morning, before leaving for school, she saw her little baby brother. He would become very special to Angelina for the rest of her life.

Following Michael's birth in 1936, the case worker came to announce that the government had established a Works Progress Administration program. With the WPA, as it was called, men who did not have a job would be given eight day's work a month paid by the government. The amount earned would be subtracted from the welfare allowance, thereby giving jobless men some work and putting a cash flow into the family.

Maddalena was happy since there never was any cash unless Cristoforo was around, or rarely, when Silia could spare some. Massimo accepted the work offered and when he received his paycheck, cashed it and announced to Maddalena that he was moving to the downstairs flat, keeping the money all to himself. This reduced Maddalena to utter desperation since the rations she was accustomed to receiving were now cut back and would not stretch for the entire month.

After the second month, Maddalena talked to the case worker about the problem. The case worker told her what she should do. This involved Angelina taking a day off from school to go downtown with Maddalena.

"Ma, I can't do that!" she said in shock. "I just can't miss school."

But Maddalena insisted. The street car dropped them off in front of a building named Cook County Courthouse, and they ended up in front of a door that read Court of Domestic Relations, Dept. 4A, Chicago Superior Court. This is where the case worker had directed Maddalena to go. As they entered the courtroom, Maddalena was trembling with fear. Massimo had so often threatened to kill her. Now maybe this would trigger him to finally do it. But she couldn't let her children starve—she had no alternative—there was no other way. She braced herself as she found a seat on the left side of the courtroom as she had been told to do. She did not see the murderous looks that Massimo was giving her.

"Ma," Angelina whispered, "Pa is sitting on the other side."

Maddalena did not have the courage to look. She had been told by the case worker to keep to herself and look only at the judge. When she was called up to the witness stand, her wobbly legs could hardly get her there. Angelina trembled for her.

The question was put to her, "Why are you here?" She softly responded as the case worker had coached her, "He won't give me the WPA money and I don't have enough to feed my children." With lowered eyes, fearing that at any moment Massimo would explode at her, she made her way back to her seat.

When Massimo was called up, he walked with a firm step and took the stand. When he was asked why he did not provide her with the money, he announced in a loud sarcastic tone of voice, "If she doesn't have money, how come she has a washing machine?"

The judge looked at him, astounded, and then made his pronouncement. "If you don't give her all the WPA money, you will go to jail. Dismissed!"

As they walked out, only Angelina saw the glare Massimo gave them. Maddalena, having finally broken the *acqua in bocca* she had been taught growing up, felt only fear and avoided looking at him. Expecting the worst when they got home, she was shocked that he ignored her. Apparently Massimo had felt the weight of the law and decided not to stir the waters at this time.

The following month when the WPA check arrived, he followed his usual procedure—cashed the check and moved downstairs. Nothing changed. Maddalena did not have the strength to follow through and put him in jail.

Chapter Thirty-Five

One summer, Cristoforo was working for the Wieboldt's Department Store as a construction worker. The store was about a mile from the house, resulting in a substantial savings in street car fare. After establishing himself as an outstanding worker, he asked his boss for a job for his brother-in-law, who, he added, had a large family and really needed the work. The boss, basing his decision on Cristoforo's impressive example, quickly agreed. Thus Massimo began working on the construction site for Wieboldt's, but, rather than alongside Cristoforo, he was put in another area.

After a week, Massimo fell and injured himself. Wieboldt's paid him a cash settlement, which he immediately hid in his wine cellar in a tubular object with a cover that looked like the end of a large bullet. Unbeknownst to him, Caroline discovered it when he sent her down for his pint of wine for lunch. Before she pushed the lever on the barrel to release the rich purple liquid into his bottle, her eye caught the strange object with the even stranger lid. Walking over to the 'bullet', as she later called it, she carefully and gingerly lifted the cover and found he had loosely stuffed his Wieboldt's cash settlement into it. After looking through the money, she selected a one dollar bill which she felt would not be missed. When she proudly gave it to Maddalena, she quickly said, "I took it from Pa, but I can't tell you where I got it." Maddalena was aghast. A whole dollar! A bonanza!

"Caroline, be careful. You know how he is."

"Don't worry, Ma," answered Caroline, he'll never miss it. He's got a lot of money." And from time to time, Caroline would raid 'the bullet' carefully to help her mother. Massimo never missed the money, secure in his control of his wine cellar.

Maddalena noticed that Caroline took on the job of finding ways to help her by cajoling and wheedling Massimo into giving her petty cash, which found its way into Maddalena's pocket. This was a great help since, most recently, Massimo had again cut off their credit at the grocery store. Caroline saw the desperation and anguish that this caused her mother and dedicated herself to somehow finding a way to relieve her anxiety. Caroline was the image of her mother; widow's peak, warm brown eyes, thick dark hair, and a gentle, sweet retiring nature. She stayed close to home and was quieter than Angelina or Clara. She admired Clara's outgoing, happy-go-lucky, tomboy ways, and she eagerly agreed to serve as a lookout during Clara's boy-crazy stage. She hardly got to know Angelina, who now left early in the morning and came home late in the afternoon from her job at Saint Mary's. From the time Angelina came home, she had her nose in her books until bedtime so they had little time together.

Recently, Angelina's senior teacher suggested she take the before-school preparation classes to pass the requirement for entrance into the Chicago Teachers' College. This was a city college that prepared teachers for the Chicago school system. It was free and the nun encouraged Angelina by telling her, "You will be a very good teacher." Angelina attended the before-school classes and passed the entrance requirements. At graduation she was also awarded a work scholarship to Mundelein College and a six-month scholarship to De Paul University Business School. Silia and Maddalena attended the graduation ceremony. When they returned home, Angelina announced that she was going to look for a job instead of accepting the awards.

"You need the money, Ma," she ventured.

Maddalena was shocked. It took her breath away. For a moment she could not speak. "Angelina," she finally said, "you must go to school and become a teacher. We made it up to now, and we will make it in the future."

"But Ma," Angelina interposed, "I just can't keep going to school when we need money to live."

"Well, didn't the OTSC offer you a job this summer supervising on the playground? And didn't Mr. Mathieu, the director, say he would give you more hours next year teaching piano and working in the library? Those are jobs, aren't they?" Maddalena pushed.

"Yeah, but that's not a lot of money and if I go to college I will need streetcar fare, books, and who knows what else," Angelina protested.

"And didn't the priest say the organist was leaving and you can have the organ job playing and singing the Masses every day—that's two dollars right there. And didn't he also include funerals and weddings to play for?" Maddalena continued.

Again, Angelina objected, "But that could all have to be used up for expenses for school. Besides for Mundelein College, I would have to leave home and live at the school. I won't do that. I won't leave you."

With some further discussion they agreed that Angelina would not accept the Mundelein College scholarship so that she could stay home and work part-time, go to De Paul University for six months, and then start Chicago Teachers College.

Mother and daughter felt a great sense of relief. Both wanted to move forward. Both understood the sacrifice needed to do so. Both accepted the burden to make their dreams come true.

Chapter Thirty-Six

Anna Felice and Jim were jubilant. She was pregnant. Her change of life brought her the child she'd always dreamed of. They named her Rosemary. Their Italian restaurant on Atlantic Avenue in Los Angeles was doing very well, and they bought a house in Huntington Park with land for a garden. Frankie came and went, and they were always happy to see him. He and Rosemary would become close friends. Life was good in California.

Frankie was called back to Chicago when his wife Elsie was diagnosed with cancer. They had two small children, Frances and Molli, who lived with Elsie and her parents while he was gone. Elsie had moved from Kendall Street because she could not tolerate Massimo's explosive behavior. The episode that finally pushed her into moving back to her parent's house happened late in the evening when everyone was settling in to go to bed. A bellowing voice in the street had broken up the quiet of the night.

"*Puttana!*" Massimo screamed at the top of his drunken voice. "*Puttana e tutte puttane figlie!*" Adding more volume to his voice, he yelled, "One-a these-a days I-a gonna kill the *puttana!*" No one in the awakened neighborhood would go out to do anything about it. Not daring to show her face, Maddalena began to think of ways to escape. Finally, Angelina, gathering up all her resources to overcome her fear, unable to stand the horrible voice ringing out its hateful message into the night, went out and found him lying in his drunken state off the curb in front of the house where he had tripped and fallen and either couldn't get up or wouldn't get up.

Gently, she pleaded, "Come on, Pa. Come into the house. I'll help you." It took everything she had.

"*Figlia di puttana, lascia mi!*" Massimo sputtered.

Undaunted, she tugged at his arm, "Aw, come on Pa. Come inside."

By this time Caroline joined Angelina and together they helped pull him up and maneuvered him into his bedroom. When he collapsed on the bed, they looked at each other and gave huge sighs of relief. Caroline ran off to tell her mother she was safe since he was passed-out. The neighborhood women would have much to gossip about the next day.

The following day, when Assunta heard about the episode, she hurried to Maddalena's house to comfort her. She brought Pietrina, her daughter, who had grown into a beautiful, dark haired, dark eyed girl with a lovely slim figure. Pietrina was now Angelina's '*comare*' since she had been her confirmation sponsor. After they sat at their coffee and discussed the previous evening's disaster, Maddalena brought up the news of Angelina's decision regarding college. Assunta was horrified.

"Maddalena, are you crazy? That school is one hour away, and she has to change two street cars to get there and to come home. Haven't you heard about the 'white slavery'? I would never let Pietrina do that."

Maddalena panicked. "What is the 'white slavery'?" she asked in a tight voice.

Assunta started her revelation. "Well, while young girls stand along the curb waiting for a street car, a car will pull up right to the curb, a door will open and someone will quickly snatch the girl, pull her into the car, and speed off fast. Right away they have the needle ready and they give her a shot of dope that makes her into a dope fiend. Her family never sees or hears from her again. They make her a *puttana*. Maddalena, you can't take that chance—college or no college," Assunta urged.

All the horrible pictures played out in Maddalena's mind. Her precious daughter lost to her forever. A white slave. A *puttana* on the streets. A dope fiend. Her stomach became queasy, and she began to shake. The blood drained from her face.

"*Dio mio*, no, no, no college. She can stay home in the neighborhood until she gets married. Then I'll know she's safe," she stated firmly.

After Assunta and Pietrina left, Maddalena could hardly wait for Angelina to get home from her summer job at the Off the Street Club. The moment she saw her daughter, a wave of relief washed over her and released some of her tension. Then the words tumbled out of her fast and furiously, "Angelina, no college. You can work here in the neighborhood. You cannot go to college. It's not good. You mustn't do it. Please listen to me. No college."

"What?" Angelina, stunned by this complete turnaround, asked again, "What? What happened?" She sensed the fear and horror her mother was feeling and asked, "Ma, tell me what happened. Why are you so upset?"

"Assunta told me," she replied.

"Assunta? What did Assunta tell you? Please, Ma, what did she tell you?"

Now seeing her daughter in front of her, hearing her voice, Maddalena relaxed a little and recounted what Assunta had told her. Angelina listened, horrified. Her mind raced with conflicting thoughts and emotions. Uppermost was the fear of this terrible thing happening to her, followed by a profound sadness at the possibility of losing her dream of becoming a music teacher. She switched back and forth from one to the other until she broke down in tears. Maddalena had rarely seen her daughter cry. It upset her.

"It's all right," Maddalena said in a comforting voice. "It will be better this way so you are safe," she added.

But Angelina would not be comforted. She was tortured for days. Walking home from work she began to stay as far from the curb as possible. She watched for any cars that came near to her side of the street. As she got close to Kendall Street, she returned to her custom of walking near the curb to avoid being hit by the rats that often made mad dashes out of a building, across the sidewalk, and to the street.

Maddalena also was torn by her desire to fulfill her and Cristoforo's plan to educate all the children. "What would Cristoforo do?" she asked herself. She missed his counsel.

A week later, when life returned to normal, Angelina made her announcement: "Ma, I've made up my mind. I'm going to college."

Chapter Thirty-Seven

At four years of age, Michael stood in the tiny dirt-filled yard outside the basement apartment using a small shovel to break up the hard dirt. His blond hair fell in curly ringlets around his face, and his hazel eyes actively took in the world while reflecting some inexplicable knowing quality. His sensitive face and beautiful physical features resembled a Botticelli angel. Angelina stood at the basement door watching him. She became his primary baby sitter by choice. She felt a protective surge of love as she watched him, and she would surround him with that love for the rest of her life.

One hot summer day, Michael sat on the front steps wishing he had some candy. He didn't have the penny necessary to buy it. Knowing that his father hung out at Vendu's candy store, he decided to walk down to the corner and go inside the store. The glass display case held an assortment of individual chocolates, hard candy, suckers, and paper strips with multi-colored sugar dots. These caught his eye and his mouth watered. He remembered in the past tearing off each dot, one at a time, and slowly sucking their sweet flavor. The red ones were his favorite.

"Well," Vendu said impatiently, "which one do you want?"

Michael, coming out of his dream of enjoying the sweets, answered timidly, "I'm looking for my father."

Vendu silently pointed to the back room. Michael had never been in the back room and approached it slowly. He knew his father's outbursts were fearful, but his desire for candy was stronger than his fear.

When he finally opened the door, he saw a smoky room in which several men were gathered at a large round table with playing cards in their hands. Glasses of wine—some already emptied, some almost full—stood next to the cards. He almost turned back, but his father's eye caught him and Massimo motioned him to come over. Heartened, Michael walked over and stood quietly at his father's side without speaking. One of the men looked curiously at the child and Massimo grunted, "mio figlio" (my son).

Now, his confidence totally restored, Michael quickly asked, "Pa, can I have a penny for candy?"

Without further comment, Massimo handed him the desired penny, and Michael made a fast retreat back to the candy counter. When he handed Vendu his penny and was given the long dotted paper strip of candy, he hurried out to sit on the curb and began pulling off the individual sweets, the red ones first. A sense of contentment came over him, more from his father's recognition than from the candy itself. It would be a moment he would never forget.

Three years later, on a quiet Saturday morning, Clara answered a loud knocking on the front door. Two tall men stood in the doorway, dressed in long dark coats and brimmed hats. One of them asked, "Is your father home?"

When she answered "No," they pushed past her into the house and, in stern voices, asked, "How about your mother?"

By this time the loud knocking and louder voices had brought Maddalena, the girls, and Michael, into the living room. No one spoke for a moment. The men's intimidating manner was not conducive to sociability.

One of the men flashed a badge and stated, "We're from the FBI. Some boys in this neighborhood are stealing from mail boxes, which is a federal offense. We're investigating who might be doing it." Looking directly at Michael, one of them asked in a dead, cold tone, "Is this your son?"

Maddalena could barely shape the word. "Yes," she answered. Everyone stood perfectly still, terrorized by the men's accusatory manner—*still*—as if in a dramatic portrait.

"We have to ask him a few questions," the man continued.

Standing tall over the seven-year-old, holding a pad in his hand for making notes, he let go a barrage of questions coldly shot out like bullets from a gun. "Are you Michael Chiuppi? Do you live in this neighborhood? Do you know anything about this mail theft? Did you have anything to do with it? Do you know anyone who does?"

No one moved. The law! Maddalena felt that her world was crumbling around her. She could not utter a sound. When Michael squeaked out, "I didn't do it. I don't know anything about it," his words released the immobile family members and Maddalena, quietly pleaded, "Please, he's a good boy, don't take him away."

Angelina added, "He's never been in trouble. He's always around the house. We know where he is at all times." At twenty-two, having experienced a world outside the neighborhood at college, she stalwartly defended her little brother. Though she was shaken to her roots, she would not reveal her fear to them; she would protect her family.

The two men turned to her and said, "OK, but we're going to be watching the kids in this neighborhood until we find out who's doing this." Drawing themselves up to their full height, they swaggered out the front door. As they left, the fear in the house was intense …the FBI. They each in their separate worlds felt the impact of the powerful over the powerless. This was worse than the police. This was the <u>government</u>. Once they found their voices, everyone started talking at once.

Clara said, "Ma, are they going to put us in jail?"

Michael began to cry. "Ma, I didn't do anything," he stammered.

Maddalena asked, "Michael, do you know any kids doing it?"

Finally, Angelina broke in saying, "OK everyone. Nobody's going to jail. All they did was question Michael. They have to do that to every boy in the neighborhood, not just Michael. Let's all take it easy. Everything's going to be OK."

The next day, when Andy and Angie and their children came over for *pranzo* (lunch) at 2 p.m. as was the custom, they all recounted the story as they had seen it. Michael and Bobby, Andy's son, were about the same age. After the meal, Bobby, who had picked up his father's love of baseball, said, "Hey Michael, let's go out to the empty lot and play baseball."

Michael, still fearful, turned to his mother. "Is it OK, Ma?" She, too, was still fearful, but she nodded yes and the boys were gone.

After they left, Maddalena turned to Andy and asked her son, "What do you think I should do? They may come after him again. Maybe one of the boys, trying to get in good with the FBI, might say it was Michael, even if it wasn't. I can't stand the thought of him being in reform school—and so young." Just the thought of it caused her to break down in tears.

Seeing and feeling her terror, Andy searched his mind for a solution, while everyone else lived and relived the scene. When he called out, "I got it!" the conversation ended abruptly.

"What?" Maddalena asked.

"Well," Andy began, "it's summer, right? School's out, right? So … why don't I drive Bobby and Michael to Arkansas and have them spend the summer away from the neighborhood and the city. By the end of the summer this will all be over. Uncle Cristoforo will be happy to have them, and they can enjoy the beautiful country, the clean air and the fresh spring water. Ricco can handle the painting business for the few days it will take me to go and drop them off."

The pall lifted, and everyone spoke at once. "What a good idea!" "A perfect solution! That's great!"

Maddalena was relieved. Expressing her gratitude in the way she knew best, she immediately refilled Andy's plate with another heaping mound of pasta, covering it with gravy, a sprinkling of cheese, then plopping one more meatball in the middle.

Within two days, Andy was on the road he knew so well from his past visits to take the boys to their summer in Arkansas.

Maddalena was thrilled. Her child would be with her brother in that beautiful place, out of harm's way. At that moment she lifted her eyes to the ceiling and for a change, she put her hands into prayerful mode and said, "*Gesu Cristo, grazie.*"

Chapter Thirty-Eight

The next years brought Maddalena a lessening of anxiety and fear, and a new sense of sweetness she had never before experienced. Her four daughters loved her and did everything they could to make life easier for her. Silia continued to live in the Cabrini-Green housing project with her two little girls. Angelina was doing well in college; Clara and Caroline were moving through high school. The dreams she and Cristoforo shared of educating the children were being realized in the girls. Maddalena watched them with a deep satisfaction. Clara and Caroline found little jobs during the summer and gave her whatever they earned. Angelina gave her everything she could after her school expenses. Maddalena used some of that money to occasionally buy a piece of meat for Angelina since she left the house at six-thirty in the morning and returned at nine-thirty at night. The schedule didn't leave her time to eat very well. Maddalena was relieved that sometimes Mr. Mathieu, the director of the Off the Street Club, would give Angelina a ride home at night. It helped to relieve her 'white slavery' anxiety.

Young people that Clara and Angelina met at the Off the Street Club began showing up at the house. Maddalena always welcomed them, and they fell under the spell of her sweetness and acceptance. Silia, playing the role of second mom, American style, supported the young people by planning Halloween parties, or Christmas parties, so that laughter and singing began to fill the house on Kendall Street. Maddalena loved it and could easily fall into party mode. They soon teased her into learning to sing "You Are My Sunshine." In her broken English she sang out,

> "You-a are-a my-a sun-a shine-a,
> My-a only-a sun-a shine-a,
> You-a make-a me happy,
> When-a skies-a are-a gray,
> You'll-a never-a know dear,
> How-a much-a I-a love-a you-a,
> Please-a don't-a take-a
> My-a sun-a shine-a away.

Her rendition was followed by much clapping and bravos. Her eyes, for the moment, lost their deep sadness.

Intermittently, Ricco and Frankie stopped by. Frankie was leaving to return to his job in California. Elsie was too sick to travel, so she and the children remained behind with her parents. When Ricco appeared, the young people took notice. In his recently developed intimidating posture, he announced loudly to the boys, "Ya gotta treat my sisters nice, or else!!" He loved to dominate the scene in a way that left no room for argument or doubt as to who was in charge. When he walked out of the room, he left behind a clear imprint of his presence.

Michael was still in Arkansas. When Andy picked up his son Bobby and left Michael behind according to Maddalena's instructions, Michael was devastated. He wanted to come home, but Maddalena was still haunted by the FBI experience. She feared that his coming back into the neighborhood would be disastrous. She felt more secure knowing he was with his uncle in that beautiful, peaceful place.

Maddalena loved listening to the girls' adventures at Grant Park, where on weekends they walked the three miles to the park to listen to the free concerts. They described the sparkling colored lights on the falling waters of the Buckingham Fountain; the large bandstand where they heard stars like Eddy Duchin, Lily Pons, and Van Cliburn; and the park area where they sat and ate their food, admiring the stunning architectural structures that formed Chicago's lakefront skyline. Through the girls and their friends, Maddalena was experiencing a life she never could have imagined. But, at the same time, the dark cloud of Massimo was ever present.

At school, Angelina heard about a telephone that could be installed in people's homes for free, but you had to put a nickel in it to make a call. When she talked to Maddalena about it, Maddalena was hesitant. "A nickel every time you call?" she asked.

"But Ma, we're not going to be making many calls. It's just good to have in case of emergency," Angelina informed her.

Maddalena agreed to the phone, and when Massimo saw it installed on the wall next to the middle bedroom, he grumbled as to why it was necessary. The phone lasted on the wall two weeks. One night, as Mr. Mathieu drove up to drop Angelina off from work, they found a large crowd gathered in front of the house. Clara and Caroline had been at home with Maddalena when Massimo showed up in a drunken rage.

"Where are you, *puttana?*" he yelled as he stormed into the house, looking for her. They were caught off guard and paralyzed for the moment. He lurched toward Maddalena, who ran into the middle bedroom and barred the door. As Caroline reached for the phone to call the police, Massimo tore the phone completely off the wall. Clara ran to the neighbors to make the call, while Caroline stood bravely at the bedroom door and tried to calm him.

"I'll break the door down!" he raved and stumbled into the kitchen to find something to help him accomplish his purpose. Caroline refused to move from the door, and by the time he returned, the police had arrived and took him to jail. The crowd was beginning to disperse when Angelina and her boss arrived. The telephone would not be replaced since it was only free the first time it was installed. Whether or not having spent a night in jail would have an effect on Massimo, only time would tell.

Chapter Thirty-Nine

She carried herself in a self-contained, stately manner that did not invite intrusion, moving within her island of chosen isolation as she crossed over from Cypress Street to Maddalena's house. After all, she had been born in Rome, but the rabble in this neighborhood were Siciliani, Calabresi, and Napolitani from the deep south of Italy. She would have none of them and them of her. She wanted to be called 'La Romana', and they were happy to do it in the most sarcastic, derisive way they could. After Zi Angelino died, she wanted to be closer to Maddalena.

Zi Angelino, Massimo's uncle, who had helped in the transition to the grocery store, had been ill for a long time and after his death the dark noisy apartment on Grand Avenue became unbearable for Zia La Romana. Her three boys were married and gone. She was ready for a change. As she climbed the long stairway onto the front porch, she stopped to catch her breath before approaching the door. She hoped Massimo would not be home. When Clara answered the door, instead of greeting her aunt, she shouted, "Ma, it's Zia La Romana!"

Brushing past what she considered an unruly girl, she went straight to the kitchen, where she found Maddalena rolling out the dough for the evening meal. Maddalena immediately invited her to join them. The two women filled each other in on what their children were doing and after dinner, Maddalena walked Zia La Romana home and invited her to the following Sunday's *pranzo*. The house vibrated with the energy of the gathering together of the children and grandchildren for the Sunday meal. On this particular day, Zia La Romana's son Jack stopped by after dinner with his friend Al Marshall. The girls were leaving for the Grant Park concerts, and when Jack offered to drive them they readily accepted. After the concert, they stopped for coffee, and in the next months, Al pursued Angelina.

When Angelina discovered he was divorced and had a seven-year-old child, she was dismayed. Maddalena would be upset. Angelina continued seeing him clandestinely for the next year, feeling guilty that for the first time, she was hiding an important part of her life from her mother. When they got engaged, she finally told Maddalena, who was upset—a divorced man with a child, a man with little education who worked in a defense factory, to marry her precious daughter? She could not and would not stop Angelina, but she was deeply disappointed and it was hard for her to bear.

The following months felt like an unstoppable avalanche. Clara met Tony Macaluso at the Off the Street Club, where Angelina worked. Caroline met Bob O'Connor at De Paul's Business School, and Silia met Joe Cristiano. Within one year, all of the daughters were married. Clara left for Yakima, Washington, where Tony's army duty called. Caroline left for Texas, where Bob was stationed, but Angelina and Silia remained in Chicago. Maddalena was very grateful.

Angelina graduated from college and began to teach music at the local elementary school. At the same time, she enrolled in De Paul University's Music School.

Maddalena felt it was time to get Michael, who was nine, back home. She left for Arkansas to pick him up. While she was gone, Elsie died of cancer. Frankie had not returned to see her, but wrote Maddalena to come and bring the children to California to help him raise the now motherless children.

Frances was seven years old and Molly was five, and Angelina and Al moved back into the Kendall Street home to receive them from their maternal grandparents while they awaited Maddalena's return with Michael.

A month later, when Maddalena returned with Michael, Angelina arranged for Felicetta and Assunta to be there. The three women dissolved in tears as they greeted each other. The day Maddalena left for California, they brought her food and goodies for the children for the train ride.

When it was time to leave, the little group made their way down the fourteen steps of the house, walked around the children playing in the street, crossed the empty lot, and headed for the Roosevelt Road streetcar line that would take them to Chicago's Dearborn Street railroad station.

The three children could hardly contain themselves with the anticipation of going on a train ride. They skipped in circles around the three adults, who walked too slowly and heavily to suit them. Maddalena, with Felicetta and Assunta hooked onto her arms, felt a mixture of excitement to be going to California, a fear of the unknown, and a profound sadness to be separating from her childhood friends. Sensing her emotion and their own, the two sisters drew close to Maddalena, sometimes making it hard for them to walk freely.

"Come on, Ma!" called out Michael, who had gotten ahead of the group. Running back to them, he warned, "If you don't hurry, we're gonna be late!"

When they finally reached the streetcar stop, the children ran back and forth, watching for its noisy arrival. As it approached, the three women clutched each other in one last desperate hug. Felicetta and Assunta wept as they watched them board and pull away. Maddalena felt that a part of her was being torn away. They would never see each other again. Massimo remained behind.

Angela Chiuppi

PART III

California

1945

"Go West, young man, go West."

—Horace Greeley

Chapter Forty

Frankie met Maddalena, Michael, Frances, and Molli at the Los Angeles railroad station. As they drove home, Maddalena was dazzled by the trees. Growing up surrounded by pine forests in Italy and then living with no trees at all in the Chicago neighborhood, the variety of trees in California kept her "oo-ing and aah-ing." She loved them all—the palm trees, the pepper trees, the eucalyptus and the jacaranda. But her favorite was the palm trees with their graceful green fronds bending in the breeze. She was drawn to the ones that seemed to hold golden balls hanging from their upper trunk. She loved the pepper trees with their full-bodied leafy branches arching away from the trunk as if to embrace the world below. The eucalyptus with its strange scaly trunks intrigued her. And the jacaranda astonished her with its clusters of purple flowers surrounded by lacy green leaves.

She was also struck by how prolific the vegetation was. Trees and bushes were everywhere. At home in Chicago, there were no trees, no bushes, no blades of grass—just buildings, houses, sidewalks, and the street. As they drove the Los Angeles streets, she felt concerned about the number of cars that Frankie had to weave in and out of, fearing that, at any time, they could have an accident. Not many cars came down Kendall Street and the family had never owned a car.

The children were fascinated by the many interesting views of the city. It wasn't flat like Chicago. You could look in different directions and see hills, almost like having pictures on the walls of a home.

As they drove out of the downtown area into the suburbs, the children, tired from the long train ride, became restless and asked, "Are we there yet?"

Frankie answered, "Relax. We have a ways to go."

After awhile, one of the children asked, "What are those black things going up and down all the time? They're all over the place."

"Those are oil derricks," explained Frankie. "They pump oil that we use in our cars." Fascinated, the children amused themselves watching the motion of the oil derricks.

"We're here," Frankie finally announced.

Maddalena looked out the window to see the Houghton Park housing project in Long Beach, California. Before her were block upon block of military-like modular trailers resembling boxcars. There were no trees or bushes here. Children were scurrying around in all directions. Clothes flapped in the breeze on clothes lines stretched out between the trailers. They pulled up beside one of the trailers, and the children happily tumbled out of the car, grateful to be able to stretch and run after their long hours of confinement.

The trailer was very small for three children and two adults. Maddalena was disconcerted—after the big house they had left in Chicago, how would she manage in such a small space? Frankie's job as a truck driver took him away from home for long stretches of time. Whenever he was in town, he took the children to visit Anna Felice and Jim.

As time passed, Maddalena felt the loss of her friends Felicetta and Assunta, the loss of her adult children, and the Italian community in Chicago. When she realized the schools were inadequate and there were no Catholic schools available, she talked to Frankie about sending the two older children to Angelina, who was now living in Butte, Montana. "She'll put them in good schools and she knows how to help them."

Frankie readily agreed and, with Angelina's acceptance, Michael and Frances were sent to Montana to live with Angelina and Al.

A friend of Frankie's told him that a lot was for sale on Platt Avenue in Lynwood, a lot that had a ramshackle house on the back with space for another house to be built in the front. One could live in the back house while in the building process. The trailer in Houghton Park had become so difficult, even with Michael and Frances gone, that Frankie jumped at the chance to build something they could all be comfortable in. He would do much of the work himself and would ask Cristoforo to come out and help.

Behind the house there was a school, a large park, and Saint Francis Hospital. The building went well, and in the meantime, Andy moved to California and bought a small house on Burton Avenue not far from the building site on Platt Avenue. He added his painting skills when the exterior was finished. Massimo arrived, having been forced to sell the house in Chicago to the state when the slum area was razed to build medical school facilities for the University of Illinois. With everyone's help the house was finally ready, and Frankie and his family, with Maddalena, moved in.

At the end of the school year Michael and Frances came home, and Michael entered the local high school. Maddalena was happy to have her children and grandchildren with her again. Her happiness was doubled when Clara and Tony moved into the Burton Street house and Andy moved on to Diamond Bar, a suburb of Los Angeles. Eventually Caroline and Bob moved in with her on Platt Avenue, leaving only Silia and Ricco in Chicago.

Chapter Forty-One

Maddalena's happiness was destroyed when news came from Chicago that the cervical cancer Silia had been diagnosed with two years earlier had spread to her bones and she was now in the terminal stage. Maddalena was crushed to be so far away and not able to help her daughter. She thought about going back to Chicago, but Caroline urged her not to rush into anything. Each day she felt like a sliver had planted itself in her heart, and she agonized over how to help her first child—the child who had been born to her in Italy when she was barely sixteen and who had opened up a new world of love for her.

When Joe, Silia's new husband, found a job in Huntington Park, California, Maddalena was elated. When they arrived, mother and daughter looked at each other—their first meeting in two years. Silia saw the gray that had begun to streak Maddalena's thick dark hair, the shoulders still crunched up toward her ears, the older face that had never lost its sweetness, and the eyes that carried the lifetime of sadness she endured. Her heart hurt for her mother. She had missed her so much, and now she was presenting her with a new burden. For a moment she wished they had not moved.

Maddalena saw the devastation of the illness and how it had reduced her daughter in every way. The face was haggard, imprinted with the constant pain she bore. The body was bent and she had lost half her weight. Her movements were slow and deliberate. Maddalena's heart cried out for her daughter. They embraced and held each other for a long time.

After the newcomers were settled in their new home, Maddalena began to call Silia every morning to check on her, which irritated Massimo. He paced around her, grumbling, "Talk, talk, talk! Every day! Every day! Talk, talk, talk!" She could hardly carry on a conversation with her sick daughter. Eventually, she complained to Angelina, who was now living in Tacoma, Washington.

"Throw him out!" Angelina said quickly and angrily. "You don't have to take that any more. It's not his house. He's got money. He can find a place to live. It's not right to take anything from him anymore."

Wanting more support and hesitant to confront him, Maddalena asked, "Do you think I should?"

"Look, Ma," Angelina continued, "he took all the money from the sale of the house when the state tore down our neighborhood to build the Medical Center. He can use that money to find a place to live. I'm sure he was smart enough to put it in the bank. He doesn't have 'the bullet' to hide it in any more. Did he give any of it to you? No! On top of that, he had a woman living with him in our house! Ma, it's time for you to be at peace. Besides, Silia needs you. Please, Ma! Do it! He can't hurt you anymore. He knows he'll go to jail." In despair, she urged her mother to make the break.

"I will," Maddalena replied in a tentative voice.

As a last desperate attempt to push her, Angelina said more quietly, "Ma, Silia needs you. You can't let him come between you and your daughter. Silia is fighting for her life. Put her first. Tell him he has to leave. Have courage. Do it."

That did it. Maddalena, thinking of the daily haranguing that kept her from staying in touch with Silia, answered, "I promise you. I will do it tomorrow when he starts with me about the phone."

The next day, when she made her call, he began interrupting her with his usual, loud, constant, ranting. Remembering Angelina's words, and encouraged by the memory that he had spent a night in jail for tearing out the phone; Maddalena now thought only of her dying daughter and her resolve strengthened. She hung up the phone and spoke as forcefully as she could.

"*Vattene da questa casa subito, questa non e' la tua casa. Vattene oggi!*" (leave this house, this is not your house, leave today) she said. Trembling inside with fear that was almost overcoming her courage, she waited for his response.

The morning California sun flooded the living room. The two figures seemed frozen in time—she, sitting by the telephone, and he, standing in the middle of the room. The moment for both of them was suspended, stretching from a second to an eternity. The *acqua in bocca* was destroyed forever.

"*Va fan gool!*" (go f*** yourself) Massimo shouted as he left the room.

Maddalena sat shaking, stunned at what she had done. When she was again able to control her hands, she picked up the phone and dialed her daughter.

Several weeks later, Massimo called Anna Felice from a trailer where he was living in Long Beach. When Anna Felice heard the news, she was furious. "Maddalena has her nerve! Throwing my brother out of the house!" she stormed.

"Rosamaria," she called to her daughter, "we must go and get him and bring him here." Rosemary was out of high school and working full-time in the restaurant. They drove to Long Beach and found him in a trailer living with a black woman. Anna Felice was livid with him. In no uncertain terms she laid down the law. "You're coming to live with me without that *puttana*, but first you give me your bank book before you lose everything you have!"

Massimo had never prepared a meal for himself, nor had he ever washed his own clothes. He had lived within a rigid routine, served always by others. His breakfast consisted of raw egg yolks blended with his usual shot of Fernet-Branca. His lunch was expected exactly at noon. If it was not ready, he pounded the table, roaring "Where is my lunch!" This was followed by a nap, a walk, beer and peanuts, and later a game of bocce in the park. His dinner, again, had to be served exactly at the same time every day. In between he sat in his rocker and puffed on his pipe.

The trailer was restrictive and the woman did not cook Italian food. The offer Anna Felice made would put him back in his routine. Releasing his bank book to her, he packed his possessions and was ready to leave. He lasted three months before Anna Felice wanted no more of him and suggested that he return to Maddalena's. When Rosemary drove him to Platt Avenue in Lynwood to drop him off, Maddalena was not there.

Maddalena had moved in with Silia to take care of her. The hospital had informed Silia that they could not keep her during an extended terminal illness. She would have to find someone that they would authorize to give her the morphine shots she needed to ease her pain. She would be released as soon as someone was found.

Maddalena struggled with this new dilemma. She knew she could not do it, her hands would shake. Angeline, Silia's first daughter, lived with them while her husband was overseas, but she had a three-year-old daughter Diane and a six-week-old baby Pat to care for, so Angeline could not do it either. As they talked over the problem, Silia said, "I want Angelina."

It was February, 1951. Clouds hovered in the Tacoma sky, pregnant with rain. Angelina had just come home from her teaching job and was talking to Frances, Frankie's daughter, and Al Junior, Al's son. Frances was living with them and when the phone rang, she answered it.

"It's for you. It's Grandma," she said and handed Angelina the phone.

"How is she?" Angelina immediately asked.

"Very bad," Maddalena answered. "I don't know what to do. They won't keep her in the hospital anymore because they say she may be sick for a long time, and there is nothing more they can do for her. They want someone at home to give her the pain shots. She is asking for you to come to do it. Could you come? Soon?"

Without hesitation, Angelina answered, "I will be there as soon as I talk to Al and take a leave from my job."

After arranging for Frances to attend the local Catholic boarding school and giving notice to her job, she bid her family goodbye to answer the call from her dying sister. "I'll be back soon," she told them. It would not be soon. It would be four and a half months later.

When she arrived in Huntington Park, Maddalena greeted her with tears in her eyes. "Silia's coming home today. A nurse will be with her and will teach you how to give the shots. Oh, Angelina, she is so very very sick. What can we do?" She choked on her words.

"It will be OK, Ma. We'll help her all we can. We have to be strong for her," Angelina answered soothingly.

But when they brought Silia home, all of Angelina's strength drained out of her. This was a shadow of the 'Little American Mother' who had always tried to make life better for her younger sisters. They brought her home on a gurney and carefully placed her on the bed. The nurse showed Angelina the procedure for measuring out and administering the morphine. After the nurse left, they were on their own.

The next four and a half months went at a snail's pace as day after day Maddalena focused on keeping her daughter alive with eggnog and chicken soup, and Angelina focused on keeping the pain at bay, sleeping in the same room with her sister to be available during the night if it became unbearable. The morphine did not help enough. They increased it and yet she wailed "*O, Dio!*" in Italian.

Maddalena felt each cry as a knife piercing her heart. She could hardly stand the torment of watching her first child leave the world in the excruciatingly slow progression of this terrible disease. The relentless screams of pain ringing throughout the house and shattering the quiet of the night tore Maddalena apart. On some evenings, she and Angelina sat in the back yard and wept together, waiting for the next cry to bring them back into the house.

They gave each other strength by focusing on the moment-to-moment requirements to keep Silia nourished and comfortable. Inexorably, the disease took its toll. She weighed only eighty-eight pounds, and the open sores on every joint of her body hardly responded to the careful 'donuts' Angelina fashioned to release their pressure on the bed.

When it was over, Angelina took the exhausted Maddalena to Tacoma, Washington, with her. They comforted each other the best they could, but Maddalena stopped talking and eating. She could not sleep. If she did, she woke up with a start hearing "*O Dio!*" ringing in her ears. She was inconsolable. Angelina became frightened for her. She tried to get her to take a tranquilizer or sleeping pills, but Maddalena would have none of it. Eventually, the darkness of the Northwest climate drove her back to California. She had gotten used to the sun.

Chapter Forty-Two

Arriving back at Platt Avenue, Maddalena found Massimo again living in the house. She was too spent to deal with the situation, and besides, the worst that could happen to her had already happened. She ignored him, and he now ignored her. Caroline and Bob and their five children moved in, and Maddalena was happy to have her children and grandchildren around her.

The grandchildren adored Maddalena. She always had a smile for them and spoke to them with a soft tone of voice. Massimo, however, was distant and grumpy, and the boys thought he was mean. They loved to play tricks on him. One of their favorites was to empty his pipe while he took his nap. They then chopped up rubber bands, mixed in a little powder from one of the bullets they had in their .22 rifles, placed the mixture in the pipe, and refilled it with the tobacco. The foul smell of the burning rubber and the hissing of the burning gunpowder enraged Massimo.

"You Goddamina somanabitcha! Amma gonna killa-a you!" he yelled as he tried to chase them down with a broomstick while they ran away laughing. Other times they put a ripe tomato under the towel he kept on the plastic chair where he liked to sit in the back yard. When he sat down, he felt the splat of the tomato and again, he jumped up and cursed them.

Frankie had now found a piece of land in Bakersfield that his new wife, Louise, wanted to build on, and he decided to move. Molli asked to stay with Maddalena and everyone agreed to it. At the same time Michael decided to join the Navy.

With Caroline and her family running the house, and no small children to care for, Maddalena, approaching sixty, decided to look for work so she could contribute to the family. For awhile she was a caretaker to an elderly Italian woman. When that ended, she took Molli with her and they cleaned houses. An opening in housekeeping at Saint Francis Hospital resulted in her getting the job, and she became the favorite of the nurses and patients. Walking through the park to the hospital was pleasurable. Life became calm and predictable. But the peace didn't last. Frankie was gravely ill and not expected to live.

"Oh! No!" Maddalena gasped. "Caroline, he's only forty-one years old, what could be wrong?"

They hurried to Bakersfield, arriving just in time. Two days later, Frankie died of kidney failure. He was the six-foot, strapping son who could not sit still. He was the only son who carried Maddalena's widow's peak and black hair. "Did the malnutrition he suffered as a child undermine his health?" she questioned herself. It was torture to think of it.

Again, her unquenchable grief caused her to withdraw from her family. They struggled to help her, but to no avail. Her children had always been her life, and now she had lost two of them at an early age. Months later she returned to her job at Saint Francis Hospital. Helping others assuaged some of her sadness as she spread her love wherever she went. People there had learned that she could sing "You Are My Sunshine," and both patients and staff teased her into performing. For a long time after Frankie's death, she begged off but one day a patient coaxed her long enough so she tried, but she broke down at "Please don't take my sunshine away." The tears flowed as she remembered her two sunshines that had been taken away.

At sixty-three, exhausted and debilitated, Maddalena found that she could not keep up with the demands of her job. She asked for a leave. Clara suggested some time visiting her and the children.

"Go Ma," Caroline urged, "it will be good for you to rest and have a change."

They drove her from Lynwood to La Verne where Clara lived with her seven children. The visit was short-lived. Two days later, Maddalena woke up, short of breath, and went into the living room to sleep sitting up in the reclining chair. At four in the morning, the strange sounds coming from her awakened Clara. Maddalena was rushed to the hospital with a heart attack followed by a stroke.

The next year was a torment for everyone. Her right side was paralyzed; her speech was garbled. Her right arm hung limply at her side. It was difficult to feed herself with her left hand. At seventy-nine years of age, after fifty years of cruelty, Massimo finally showed a small sign of sympathy. He reached over to try to help her feed herself. She pushed his hand away and glared at him. As time went on, she made a huge effort to get around by herself by planting her left foot firmly and slowly pulling her bad leg forward. It was to no avail. By the end of the year, she was back in the hospital with another stroke. Saint Francis' staff welcomed her by returning her love with the best care they could give her. Angelina flew down from Washington, and Ricco from Chicago, to join their brothers and sisters at her bedside.

She floated in and out of consciousness. At times the stricken faces of her children flashed before her, but they seemed so far away and, though she struggled mightily, she could not communicate with them. Suddenly she was back in the piazza chasing the birds or guarding Cristoforo. When she heard the voice of her childhood nurse, Giuseppina, calling to her, she felt the warm sand under her feet as she ran freely along the Adriatic shore... she was finally at peace.

Epilogue

Cristoforo Ferrara died at 72 of a heart attack in Three Brothers, Arkansas.

Massimo Chiuppi died at 92 from complications of pneumonia, having lived alternately with his daughters Clara and Caroline in California.

Anna Felice Mansoli died at 91 from complications of surgery in Huntington Park, California.

Afterword

The story of Maddalena is also my story. In my ninety-third year, the perspective given by age and maturity allows me to look back as though through a crystal ball in reverse. The ball of yarn is unraveled and re-knitted into the true story of a heroic woman who fought on the battlefield of poverty and abuse at a time when women had no choice—a woman who strove to feed and clothe her children, to educate them and keep them safe in a risky environment, a woman whose indomitable spirit revealed her depth of character and her capacity for courage and love. This is the legacy she left to her children, grandchildren, and those who follow. The journey for me has been emotionally wrenching. But today I am a long way from the bitter winters and the squalor of the slums of Chicago's Near West Side.

The final chapter of my life is set in a sweet little house on a hill facing a view of mountains and sky above a steep slope planted with fruit trees, and a graceful statue standing in the middle of a pond full of fish and water lilies. No rats. No cockroaches. No bedbugs. No lice. A gift to enjoy.

More than that—my heart is filled with forgiveness for Massimo. The clouds of fear and hatred for his abuse of Maddalena and the neglect of his family are lifted by the understanding and compassion I have developed through the process of writing this book. He knew not what he did.

I am grateful that in the midst of her winter and mine, my mother left in me her invincible summer. The debt the family and I owe you, Maddalena, is beyond measure. "Thank you, Ma."

Acknowledgments

The first line of this book was written in December 1999 and the last line in December 2011. That it took twelve years—squeezing itself into a busy schedule of teaching singing, studying piano, organizing bi-annual recitals for my students, and performing the necessary mundane activities of daily life—is not surprising. That it was at all possible is due to the support and encouragement of many people. Working through my eighties and early nineties, I was fortunate to find my friend and amazing doctor, James A. Novak, MD, who not only kept me healthy with his integrative medicine techniques, but also supported my goal with his faith and his persistent pushing to "finish the book."

In the writing of the book itself, first and foremost I owe everything to my son and friend, Christopher David Marshall. As my editor-in-chief, his literary skills turned words and phrases into more coherent expressions. His efforts to transfer my handwritten pages into the computer created a legible manuscript to work from. His dogged patience in ferreting out repetitive phrases and redundant words crafted the story to a higher level. Above all, his unfailing belief in the book and his "Keep writing Mom," sustained me through these many years. Thank you, Chris.

The book might have been stillborn as a manuscript had it not been for my patient "midwife agent," Jo Ann Wood O'Connor and her husband, Robert O'Connor, who teamed up to take over the responsibility of handling all the details with the publisher. I owe them an unpayable debt of gratitude for their love and support. In addition, the hours they spent offering critical editing skills and photographic 'know-how' were indispensible to the completion of the final product.

To Judi Patterson, my friend and colleague, there is no sufficient way to express my thanks for her profound sensitivity to the story and her keen insight into the development of the structure and alignment of the characters. Also, with her detailed editing ability and her merging of the necessary revisions into the computer, she advanced the progress of the book. Utilizing the skills of her thirty-year career as a creative writing teacher made her contribution invaluable.

I offer my gratitude to my grand-niece, Ann Marie Maher, who from the beginning not only supported the book, but also offered her phenomenal editing skill and her beautiful photographs of Italy. She went through the manuscript with painstaking detail bringing more clarity to the reader. My dearest friend, Caroline Reginato Hamlin, was a deep well of consistent, unfailing emotional support. Her background as an English teacher and lover of good literature offered editing skills that moved the book along.

The research necessary to piece together Maddalena's life in Italy was only possible because of the generosity and support of my niece and nephew, Genine and Richard Macaluso, who subsidized my many trips to Italy. Their assistance in discovering places and people for interviews and information ignited their passion for Italy as it sparked my excitement to fill in the details of Part I in the book. *Grazie, Riccardo e Giannina!*

Thank you to my readers who offered suggestions and support: my niece Annie Maher; my students Stella Saling, Lynette Heitman, Michele Manker, Pauline Rippel, Adele Campbell, and my dear friend, Lois Moe. To my student, Mary Summerday, thank you for your work on the front cover.

Thanks also go to my neighbor, Kalisa Wells, who kept me supplied with fresh organic fruits and vegetables and who, at crucial times, brought me exquisite meals, befitting her love of cooking and her skills as a professional chef. When asked to look at the manuscript, Kalisa generously spent days tenaciously studying its ingredients and made a major improvement to the recipe for *Maddalena*. Thank you for your love and faith in the book.

Dennis Selder came late to the manuscript and offered his enormous professional skill and insights. Thank you Dennis.

A word of gratitude for my health team: Dr. Kevin Stevens,

chiropractor, Jeffrey Kroll, acupuncturist, and Jennifer Walker, masseuse. Your love and expertise sustained me.

All of the above took the book to their hearts and wrapped themselves around it. For that and your love, I sing out as the king did in *Amahl and the Night Visitors*—"Thank you, thank you, thank you!"

About the Author

Angela Chiuppi is a vigorous and active 93-year-old woman whose career has been mainly in music and counseling. She holds Master's degrees in Music and in Counseling Psychology.

In her career as a public school music teacher, she led her students in a creative project in the Fine Arts, in which they wrote, produced, and successfully staged an original musical called *Sheherezade*, based on *Tales from the Arabian Nights*.

At present she is a master voice teacher, who presents her students in a recital every two years. Angela lives in La Mesa, California.

CPSIA information can be obtained at www.ICGtesting.com
Printed in the USA
LVOW111925310512

284094LV00001B/7/P